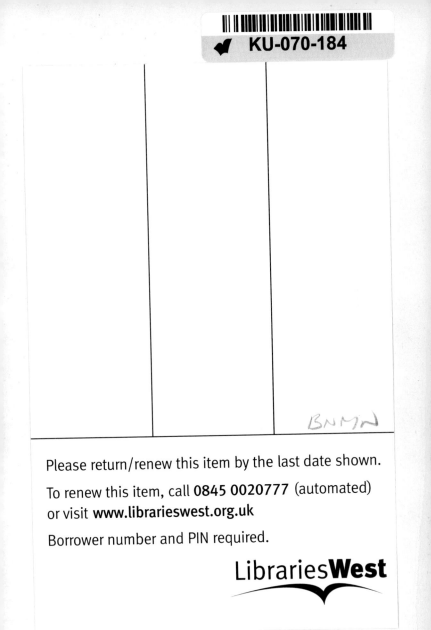

A *Seriously Useful Author's* Guide to

Writing a Marketable Book

Charlie Wilson

t

Troubador Publishing Ltd
9 Priory Business Park
Wistow Road
Kibworth Beauchamp
Leics LE8 0RX, UK
Tel: (+44) 116 279 2299
Email: books@troubador.co.uk
Web: www.troubador.co.uk

ISBN 978-178088-272-7

A Cataloguing-in-Publication (CIP) catalogue record for this book
is available from the British Library.

Typeset by Troubador Publishing Ltd, Leicester, UK
Printed and bound in Great Britain by
Clays Ltd, St Ives plc

MIX
Paper from
responsible sources
FSC® C013056

About the Author

Charlie Wilson is an author, a ghostwriter, an editor and a bookworm. She's the founder of The Novel Prize for unpublished novelists and The Book Specialist Ltd, an agency providing writing and editorial services to authors and publishers. To find out more about Charlie, and to contact her, visit www.thebookspecialist.com.

Contents

Introduction

If you're reading this book, it's no doubt because you are planning to write, or have already written, a book. Congratulations! Nothing beats the feeling of being an author (just see people's eyes light up in admiration when you tell them you've written a book). And I take my hat off to anyone who has the discipline, determination and courage to create a book.

That said, writing a book is pretty easy. You sit at a computer and type and type, or you sit on the sofa with a notebook and scribble and scribble. Anyone can write a book. But writing a *good* book, a book that sells – well, that's much harder. If you want to get published, or you want to self-publish a book and shift more than a few copies, you need to write a book that readers want to buy. A *marketable* book.

And that's where this Seriously Useful Author's Guide comes in...

What This Book Is About

When it comes to books, marketing is crucial. Publish a book and neglect to tell a soul about it and you won't sell a single copy. Sales come down to effective marketing. But for marketing to succeed, a book must be marketable in the first place.

So this book is about how to write a *marketable book*: one that can be marketed. Two key questions determine whether a book is marketable:

- Does a market exist for the book?
- Is it a decent book that readers will like?

Answer yes to both questions, and you've got a marketable book. Answer no to either, or both, and your book is unlikely to do well.

Think of it this way: If you want to self-publish, you need to be putting out *a marketable book that will sell*. If you want to get published, you need an agent and publisher to be convinced that this is *a marketable book that will sell*. Whatever path you take, marketability is key.

Who This Book Is For

This book is for anyone who's writing, or has written, a book and who cares about selling that book – whether to a publisher or directly to the reader via self-publishing.

If you've written a book for the sheer joy of the writing process and you've no interest in publishing it, or you want to get it printed just to give copies to your family, that's fine. Put this book down now and go back to enjoying your writing.

But if, like the vast majority of authors, you're writing a book because you want to publish it and sell lots of copies, this guide is essential reading.

Writing a Marketable Book applies to all types of author:

- Male authors[*]
- Female authors
- Unpublished authors
- Experienced authors
- Authors seeking an agent/publisher
- Self-publishing authors
- Ebook authors
- Print book authors
- Non-fiction book authors
- Fiction book authors[**]

Whoever you are, whatever you're writing and however you plan to publish it, this book contains information, guidance and examples to help you create a book that sells.

Why I Wrote This Book

Over the years I've worked with and met many authors. Those who have done very well with their books – getting book deals or achieving healthy sales with self-publishing – are united by one basic truth: their books are marketable.

Publishers like marketable books.

[*] I alternate between male and female pronouns in the book; but all content is of course relevant to all readers.
[**] The focus in this guide is on writing a substantial book, but much of the advice also applies to writers of poems, short stories and books for young children.

Agents like marketable books.

Readers like marketable books.

Meanwhile, agents and publishers' slush piles are teetering under the weight of manuscripts that won't get published. Amazon is stuffed full of ebooks that sell but a few copies, and poorly written self-published books that have scathing reviews. Too many people are writing books that aren't marketable.

So, many authors aren't achieving their aspirations. And the author of a book that doesn't do well feels demoralised, despondent, frustrated.

I make it my business to encourage writers. (Don't take that to mean that I offer false hope or insincere praise. I don't. But I do have respect for anyone who has the creativity and commitment to write; and I do believe that if you want to write, you should do so – *while having realistic expectations of where that writing is going.*) So I find it concerning that so many authors I meet are struggling and unhappy. The point of writing is self-fulfilment. Writing is a joy, a release, an art. Something is going wrong if authors are feeling angry and let-down and unable to see the path forward.

I wrote *Writing a Marketable Book*, then, to offer practical guidance to authors that I think is currently lacking in the publishing industry. By following the advice in this book, you develop a considered, careful, intelligent, professional approach to writing a book. And you greatly improve your chances of creating a book that gets published and sells well.

A Brief Guide to the Book

Before diving into the book, take a look at the following sections, which give you an idea of the structure and the key features.

A Chapter Overview

Part 1 covers the thinking and planning stage that comes before you sit down and write.

- Chapter 1 helps you determine whether you've got what it takes to write a marketable book, covering talent, experience, willingness to write for a market, publishing knowledge, commitment, professionalism and realistic expectations.
- Chapter 2 introduces you to marketability within book publishing. As well as looking at the author's perspective, you consider the viewpoints of agents, publishers and readers.
- Chapter 3 is all about coming up with, and then developing, an idea for your book. The focus in this chapter is on ensuring that the idea is marketable – so you explore whether your idea is original and whether a market exists for the book.
- Chapter 4 gets you ready to write. You lay the foundations for the book, pinning down the genre and the target reader, researching and creating a synopsis, a one-line pitch, a chapter breakdown and a writing plan.

Part 2 is dedicated to non-fiction writing.

- Chapter 5 helps you come up with a great title for your book, taking you through various styles of title to help you brainstorm ideas.
- Chapter 6 delves into the content of the book, helping you write accurately and thoroughly, offering some guidance on how you come across as an author and highlighting legal issues to be aware of. This chapter also takes a look at how you write an autobiography or biography.
- Chapter 7 gives you the lowdown on structuring your non-fiction book. Information on chapters and sections, grouping information, chronology and length helps you firm up a logical, sequential, clear structure.

Part 3 focuses on writing a fiction book.

- Chapter 8 gives you plenty of ideas for coming up with a marketable title for your book, from the 'somebody-somebody-and-the-something-something' title to the 'excerpt-of-the-book' title.
- Chapter 9 focuses on the setting for your novel, exploring real and imaginary places as well as past, present and future timescales.
- Chapter 10 is all about characters, looking at the various types and levels, qualities and personalities, descriptions, names and development.
- Chapter 11 focuses on plot and structure, covering the importance of careful structuring, how you break down a story, timelines, points of view, plot threads, inconsistencies, pace and length.

Part 4 looks at how you write, considering the language side of writing.

- Chapter 12 helps you develop your command of language. You gain confidence in your craft as you consider areas like vocabulary, sentence and paragraph structuring, clarity, simplification and making every word count.
- Chapter 13 gives you a crash course in correcting common spelling, punctuation and grammar issues.
- Chapter 14 helps you apply a consistent style to your writing, from spelling and dialogue through to capitalisation and italicisation.

Part 5 gives you the tools to transform your first draft into a published, marketed book.

- Chapter 15 covers the revising and feedback stage – including editing, critiquing and proofreading. Using this chapter, you can polish your rough first draft into a book that's ready to publish.
- Chapter 16 is all about publishing your book – whether that entails submitting the book to agents and publishers, or self-publishing. I also touch on writing competitions as a route to publication.
- Chapter 17 takes a look at marketing your book, considering aspects like budget, time, author profile, pseudonyms, offline marketing and online marketing, with a view to helping you put together a marketing plan.
- Chapter 18 covers the period after publication or submission to agents/publishers. You assess the success of your book, and then decide where to go next: hopefully, writing your next marketable book.

Key Points

Through the book you'll find bold keywords introducing paragraphs that flag important points:

- **Try This:** Practical guidance you can apply.
- **Remember:** If you remember nothing else on the page, make it this.
- **Word to the Wise:** A warning; ignore at your peril.
- **Toolkit:** Denotes an item to put in your toolkit (see the later section on the toolkit).

Examples

The shaded boxes include two types of example:

- UMB example – an example of an *unmarketable* book. Most of these examples are unpublished (for obvious reasons!).
- MB example – an example from a *marketable*, published book.

Toolkit

This book helps you create an author's toolkit that contains all the information you need as you devise, plan, write, publish and market your book.

Style your toolkit however you like. You may have a Toolkit file on your PC where you place various relevant documents. You may buy a big notebook in which you write all the information. Or you may use loose sheets of paper and collate them in a box file or lever-arch file, or stick them up on a wall in your writing room.

Whatever you do, keep your toolkit up-to-date, safe and to hand. This is your writing bible.

How to Read This Book

Read this book however you like. In one sitting. A page at a time. Jumping about. Backwards. Although the book is sequential, following the writing, publishing and marketing process, each chapter stands alone. So you can read the book from cover to cover, or simply skip to the bits that most interest you.

I hope you find this book informative, helpful, inspiring and confidence-building. And if the end result of your reading is a marketable book, I'd very much like to take a look. Do let me know about your book via www.thebookspecialist.com.

Part 1

Before You Write: Thinking and Planning

1. Have You Got What It Takes?

Before you even think about writing a marketable book, be sure you've got what it takes. Being honest at this point saves disappointment further down the road. Many authors who fail to get published, or who self-publish and get poor reviews and/or sales, would have been wise to choose not to write a book in the first place. Make sure that's not you: use this chapter to check you have the necessary attributes and attitudes to write a great book.

Writing Talent

At the risk of stating the obvious, if you're going to write a marketable book, you need to be able to write!

Can you write? *Really* write? Has anyone in your life ever told you that you write well?

- No: Never? This is a bit of a worry. Before you get too carried away with dreams of creating a marketable book, I advise you to sit down and do some writing, and then ask people you trust and respect for their opinion.

- Yes: Great, that's good news. Just to check, though, we are talking about people who know their stuff here, yes? If the only person who's ever commended your writing is your mum, and all she reads is cereal packets, she's perhaps not the best judge of writing ability.

When considering writing talent, the nature versus nurture debate emerges. To what degree can you learn to be a good writer, and to what degree do you just instinctively know how to write well?

Any creative skill can be nurtured. Painting classes, music lessons, singing tuition, drama workshops – they all help students to develop. Is every student going to be the next Picasso or Jools Holland or Katherine Jenkins or Dame Judi Dench? No. Some are good; some are mediocre; some are dreadful.

You can be a successful author who's good, but not exceptional. You can be a moderately successful author who's just mediocre. But you won't make it as an author if writing doesn't come naturally to you. By all means write if you enjoy writing, but be realistic about your potential.

Writing Experience

Experience in writing is useful. How used to writing are you? Do you write in your day job? Have you written anything before that's been published – a short story, a report, a website?

If you like the *idea* of writing, but you don't actually write, I recommend you devote some time to writing now. Keeping a diary or blogging is a great way to get into a regular writing habit.

A Desire to Write a Book for a Market

Recently, I was talking to a group of authors.

'What are you writing at the moment?' one wanted to know.

'A book about writing a book,' I replied.

'Sounds interesting. What's the angle?'

'Well, it's about writing a book that's marketable – so you think about the marketability of your book before and while writing it.'

'Gah! Sounds horrendous,' was the diplomatic response. 'I write for *me*. I write the stuff I want to read. I can't bear the idea of deliberately writing to please a publisher or reader. Surely you end up with trashy books pedalled out to a formula? Where's the authenticity and creativity in that? Writing is an art, not a business venture.'

'Thanks for your input,' I said with as warm a smile as I could muster. 'I meant to ask you, how are you getting on with your book?'

'Well, I've sent it out to seventy agents and publishers now. No joy yet.'

'Oh dear. Well, good luck with it!'

Every book you write is for yourself, of course. Otherwise there would be no point writing it. You have to connect to the book and believe in its worth. You have to enjoy writing it and feel passionate about every word. But if you want your book to *sell*, you also have to consider the marketability of your book before, and as, you write. Otherwise you can quite easily write an unmarketable book whose only reader will be yourself. And perhaps your Aunt Ethel.

The author who was having kittens about writing a marketable book had made an assumption: that a marketable book is formulaic, and therefore writing one stymies creativity and individuality.

Some marketable books are written very deliberately to mirror existing published books that have done well. They're either following a tried-and-tested formula, such as a Mills & Boon romance, or they're slotting into a current fad in publishing (see the section 'Chasing a Trend' in Chapter 3). But such books make up only a small proportion of marketable books.

Remember: A marketable book is fresh and original, but it's based on a clear understanding of what publishers/readers want and like.

A Good Understanding of Publishing

If you want to write a marketable book, you can't write in a vacuum. You need to know your market, and you need to know about the business of publishing.

Don't worry; I don't expect you to be an expert on the publishing industry. But the more you know, the better. So you need to be prepared to put some effort into learning. Chapter 2 gives you a good grounding in the basics of marketability and publishing.

Commitment to All Stages of the Process

Writing a book takes a great deal of commitment. Your novel

or non-fiction title will take many hours to write.

But beyond sitting at a computer typing away or scratching out words in a notebook, there's a whole lot more to writing a marketable book. Before you have a complete manuscript, you've got to:

- Read widely in the genre.
- Come up with, and develop, a great idea.
- Research the book.
- Plan the book.
- Write the book.
- Revise the book – over and over.
- Proofread the book.

That gets you to the point of having a finished manuscript. But the fun's only just begun. If you're submitting to agents and publishers, and you get published, you've all these jobs:

- Write good submission materials.
- Send out the book over and over.
- Revise the book according to the agent's suggestions.
- Revise the book according to the publisher's suggestions.
- Work with the publisher's editor.
- Proofread the book, again.
- Help to market the book (a massive, time-consuming task).

If you're self-publishing the book, you've all these jobs:

- Commission a cover designer.
- Commission a typesetter.
- Handle the self-publishing company, or handle the publishing process yourself.

- Proofread the book, again.
- Write the blurb.
- Market the book extensively (a massive, time-consuming task).

Many authors I come across run out of steam somewhat during the long journey from deciding to write a book through to readers buying it in droves. They rather enjoy the writing side, especially as this involves being lost in a world of their own. But taking the product (their book) to market and selling it – that's another matter entirely.

If you're serious about writing a marketable book, you've got to commit to every part of the process. It's a hell of a lot of work, but as a midwife pointed out to me while I was in labour with my son, 'the best things in life don't come easy'.

Professionalism

The very fact that you're reading this book tells me you've at least some business acumen. Great; you're going to need it.

This is the unprofessional approach that some authors expect they can take:

You write a book. You don't think about anyone but yourself as you write. It's all for you. You hand the finished manuscript over to a publisher, who publishes the book exactly as you wrote it. You have nothing more to do with the book – the publisher takes care of everything. Straight away, locked in your writing room, you get stuck into the next book. You write and write, and surface now and again to read an email that tells you that your book is selling phenomenally well.

Alternatively:

You write a book. You don't think about anyone but yourself as you write. It's all for you. You self-publish the finished manuscript. You don't bother with marketing; that's too scary or too complicated or too business-sounding or too time-consuming or simply beneath you. Straight away, locked in your writing room, you get stuck into the next book. You write and write, and surface now and again to check your Amazon sales figures. Another 10,000 copies sold.

This is the reality if you follow the unprofessional approach:

You write a book. You don't think about anyone but yourself as you write. It's all for you. You hand the finished manuscript over to a publisher. The publisher says, 'Thanks, but no thanks.'

Alternatively:

You write a book. You don't think about anyone but yourself as you write. It's all for you. You self-publish the finished manuscript. You don't bother with marketing; that's too scary or too complicated or too business-sounding or too time-consuming or simply beneath you. Straight away, locked in your writing room, you get stuck into the next book. You write and write, and surface now and again to check your Amazon sales figures. One copy sold. Oh, and the buyer's written a stinking review.

This, on the other hand, is the professional approach – the one that sells books:

> *You write a book. You think carefully about marketability before, while and after you write it. You submit the finished manuscript to a publisher, along with a great synopsis and covering letter that shows the book has a market and you've some good ideas for marketing. The publisher revises the book with you, to improve marketability. You spend the following months, even years, working closely with the publisher, helping the marketing team and doing lots of marketing activities yourself – book tours, literary festivals, blogging, tweeting, local radio interviews. You try to squeeze in writing the next book when you can, thinking carefully about marketability before, while and after you write it.*

Alternatively:

> *You write a book. You think carefully about marketability before, while and after you write it. You self-publish, taking care that the book is of a professional standard to compete with traditionally published books. You devise a well-thought-out marketing strategy and you spend the following months, even years, doing lots of marketing activities – book tours, literary festivals, blogging, tweeting, local radio interviews. You try to squeeze in writing the next book when you can, thinking carefully about marketability before, while and after you write it.*

The published authors I know who've done well have one thing in common: professionalism.

Writing is a creative pursuit. Publishing is a business. Separate the two in your mind and you'll do well.

Books are products. The same as shaving foam and sofas and saucepans. Books are things that a manufacturer (the publisher) creates to sell to a retailer (the bookshop) to sell to a consumer (the reader). If you want a book to sell well, therefore, you have to apply all the same business and marketing knowledge to book creation as you would to creating and selling any other product.

Try This: If you're not au fait with the business world, watch an episode of *The Apprentice*. It's a terrifying, and in many ways overblown, representation of how business works because the contestants are so aggressive, but it does get you thinking about the whole point of creating products to sell.

Remember: Publishers and agents love professional authors, because they know they're hardworking, sensible and good to work with. They don't love airy-fairy, precious authors who float about without a clue how the business world works. Life's just too short to spend it trying to rein in a prima donna or off-the-planet, thesp-type author.

UMB examples: The unprofessional approach

- In your covering letter you tell an agent/publisher that you've

written 'the next *Harry Potter*'.
- You fully expect to buy a castle in Scotland with the profits from your book.
- You can't take constructive criticism.
- You can't or won't set aside lots of time for your book.
- You're unwilling to be involved in marketing.
- You think the following sentence is great writing: *It was a big adventure what I liked specially the bit with the gynormous very big rat thing but then i realised it was all just a dream… I mean I dreamed the hole story, can you belief it?*

Realistic Expectations

Once upon a time, the writer was a frightfully creative, impoverished *artiste* scribbling away in a drafty garret, reconciled to the fact that he wrote because he loved to, not because it made him a decent income. Fast-forward to recent years, and the cult of the celebrity and the phenomenal success of a handful of authors has led to people dreaming of being a published author because they think it will *make them rich and famous*. Time for a reality check.

Traditional publishing:
- The vast majority of authors who submit a book to agents/publishers don't get published.
- Of those who do get published, the vast majority don't make enough money from their book(s) to be a professional (full-time) author.
- Of those who are professional authors, the vast majority

don't make enough money to have a luxurious lifestyle.
- The verdict: Only a very tiny proportion of published authors are rich and famous.

Self-publishing:
- The vast majority of authors who self-publish don't sell a huge number of books.
- Of those who do sell a decent number of books, the vast majority don't make enough money from their book(s) to be a professional (full-time) author.
- Of those who are professional authors, the vast majority don't make enough money to have a luxurious lifestyle.
- The verdict: Only a very tiny proportion of published authors are rich and famous.

Some rich and famous authors are rich and famous because they're amazingly talented. Some rich and famous authors are rich and famous despite the fact they're *not* amazingly talented. And for every rich and famous author that exists, there's another out there who's fabulously talented but isn't catching a break.

So many factors affect whether an author does well; it's not just about the writing. Luck, timing, public reaction and need at a point in time – all these play a part. No one can quite pin down why exactly *Harry Potter* and *Twilight* have become international sensations. Millionaire self-published author Amanda Hocking has some suggestions for why her books have sold so well – popular genre, decent covers, low price, recommendations from bloggers – but she has no definitive recipe for success.

I'm not telling you this to depress you. Of course you should dream of yachts and mansions and attending award ceremonies wearing Versace if that's what motivates you. But be clear about the chances of living that dream. The proceeds from your first book may buy you a Hot Wheels car (99p), a remote-controlled car (£30), an old banger (£300), a pre-loved Mini (£1,000) or a new Ford Fiesta (£8,500), depending on how well it sells, but they're really unlikely to stretch to a Ferrari (£200,000).

Word to the Wise: Check your motives for writing. If writing a book is simply a passport to wealth and notoriety, give up now. Apply to a reality TV show instead. If you want to write a book, make it because you eat, breathe and sleep writing; because being a writer is a big part of who you are; because your dream is to share your writing with the world.

In a Nutshell

- Know that you can write before trying to write. Make sure that the diamond in the rough isn't in fact a speck of beer-bottle glass.
- Write for a reader if you want to sell to a reader.
- Know lots about publishing.
- Realise that creating a marketable book is about a lot more than just writing.
- Take a professional approach.
- Be prepared to work hard.
- Don't write because you think it'll make you rich and famous.
- Write because you love to write.

2. Understanding Marketability

Chapter 1 helps you establish that you've got what it takes to write a marketable book. But what exactly is a marketable book? Before you launch into the book creation process, you need a good understanding of what marketability means when it comes to book publishing.

Defining Marketability

A marketable book is one that can be successfully marketed. For a book to be marketable, it must:

- Have a market.
- Please that market.

So you need a good book that readers want to read.

Some books are highly marketable. For example, a premiership footballer's memoir can be successfully marketed because there's a large existing market for the book, and the book will please the readers by giving them what they want: an insight into the guy's private life.

Some books are marketable, but on a less impressive scale. For example, a guide to London is marketable to tourists coming to London and it pleases them by delivering the information they require.

It's worth noting that some badly written books are

marketable. I once read an autobiography of a famous British comedian and was horrified by the quality of the writing (it had been ghostwritten in a rush, I think). I certainly wasn't pleased by the book. Still, the book sold very well – despite negative reviews.

Word to the Wise: Don't be inspired by the shoddy-writing-sells example. Unless you're hugely famous and people will read your book just because it's *your* book, you have to write well.

Why Care About Marketability?

Because if you don't, you're not going to sell many books.

Your response to this may be, 'I don't care. I just want to write.' Okay then. Nothing wrong with that. Put this book down and go and write.

But if you're bothered about selling copies of your book, you've got to think about the market.

Standing in the Competition's Shoes

Think about all the authors you're competing against with your book.

•   If you're looking to get published, think about how many other authors are also trying to impress agents and publishers. Each year, literary agents and publishers receive huge numbers of submissions. Most have a person whose entire job consists of reading submissions. At a recent conference for authors that I attended, a literary agent explained that his agency had received 4,900 submissions the previous year. Of the submissions, the agent's reader had passed 150 to the agents to review. The agents had been interested in 50. They sold three to publishers.

- If you're self-publishing, you're one of many thousands of people who'll do so this year. And you're not just competing with other self-published authors; your book is up against all books already published and those that publishers will publish this year. As a guide, in 2011, 149,800 books were published in the UK (2,000 in Ireland and 2,385,100 in the rest of the world), and the ISBN Registration Agency for the UK and Ireland issued 3,412 new publisher prefixes (source: Nielson).

So there are lots and lots of authors out there who also want to be published and sell lots of books.

What's going to make you succeed against this competition? How can you stand out in a very crowded marketplace? These are the questions you need to keep in your mind when creating and publishing your book – these are the questions at the heart of marketability.

Standing in the Agent's Shoes

The literary agent is the gatekeeper of the publishing world. Although some publishers are open to direct submissions from authors, many – particularly the giants of publishing – only accept books that come via a literary agent.

Many authors grumble about literary agents. These are the complaints I hear:

- They're snooty.
- They're old-school.
- They're too scared to take on anything new.
- They have too much power.
- They're too slow.
- They don't bother to give feedback.

Distrust is a common theme. I get told pretty often, 'JK Rowling was rejected by twelve agents.' Subtext: literary agents haven't a clue what they're doing. Actually, as far as I understand it, Rowling was signed by the second agent she approached, who then sent the book out. It was rejected by twelve *publishers* before Bloomsbury took the book. So she didn't struggle much to get an agent.

Here are some things you need to realise about agents:

- They're good at spotting good books. Otherwise they wouldn't be in business.
- They know the market and the business of publishing very well.
- They genuinely want to find a book that's so good they can't put it down – the whole point of being an agent is the hunt for something fresh and exciting.
- It's not an agent's job to give you feedback on your book – if you want feedback, commission a professional editor. You're taking a product (your book) to someone who scouts for products for a company (the publisher). You're

offering them a product. They've no obligation to spend an hour or two helping you develop that product if they don't want it, or even explaining to you why they don't want it.

- To take on a book, they have to be through-the-roof passionate about it. Quite liking it isn't enough.

- If an agent takes on a book and then sends it out to editors in publishing houses, the agent is staking her reputation on the book. If she keeps sending round books that aren't quite good enough, trust in her abilities diminishes and her career heads downhill.

- Just because one agent doesn't connect to a book, doesn't mean another won't. The agents who reject an author simply didn't connect, which means they wouldn't have represented the book well. You don't want any old agent – you want one who thinks your book is utterly fabulous.

So what's an agent looking for in your book? Quite simply, the wow factor.

Remember: If an agent likes your submission, she'll request the full manuscript. If she's impressed, her next step will be to check you out – to call you and then, ideally, to meet you. Because even if she's sure you've written a great, marketable book, she needs to know that she can work with you – and that a publisher can work with you. See the later section 'Being a Marketable Author'.

Standing in the Publisher's Shoes

Publishers want a book they can sell. It's as simple as that. Publishers love books, yes; but they're businesses first and foremost, and what counts is that the products they produce to sell make them money. Therefore, publishers are only interested in marketable books.

If authors grumble about agents, they all-out moan about publishers:

- They're snooty.
- They're old-school.
- They're too scared to take on anything new.
- They have too much power.
- They're too slow.
- They don't bother to give feedback.
- They publish memoirs from rubbish celebrities, but won't publish new novels.
- They take on very few new authors.

Here are some things you need to realise about publishers:

- They're good at spotting good books. Otherwise they wouldn't be in business. But they also get it wrong sometimes. And that's costly. And it stings. So they worry about it happening again.
- Publishing a book is expensive. So they have to be confident in their investment.
- They know the market, and the business of publishing, very well.
- They genuinely want to find a great book, because that's a book that will make them money and make them look

good – and they're a business, so they're driven by profit and profile.

- They don't just want to spot potential; they want to see potential realised.
- It's not their job to give you feedback on your book – if you want feedback, commission a professional editor.
- They have no obligation to authors who submit manuscripts. There's no right to be published. You're offering a product to the publisher; if the publisher doesn't want it, that's that. It's not for those outside of a publishing company to tell it how to operate.
- To take on a book, they have to be through-the-roof passionate about it. Quite liking it isn't enough.
- We're in a recession, and the publishing industry in particular is struggling with the decline of high-street bookshops and the rise of ebooks and self-publishing. Publishers are risk-averse – so it's easier to say no than yes.
- Publishers have lists, and will reject a book they like if it doesn't fit with their list at that point. For example, if you've submitted a great young adult dystopian novel set in 19th-century London, and the publisher already has a young adult dystopian novel set in 19th-century London on its list, it's unlikely to take yours on.
- An editor in a publishing house may adore your book. But that editor has to convince other departments to buy into the book too. So the members of the sales team need to believe they can sell it. And the members of the marketing team need to believe they can market it. See how important marketability is?

So what's a publisher looking for in your book? The wow factor, and a book that looks to be a safe investment and that fits with the publisher's business situation and objectives.

Standing in the Reader's Shoes

An agent and a publisher think about what a reader wants, and this thinking is wrapped up in the decision each makes about the submission of a book. So if you're trying to get published, you need to think about the wants and needs of both the agent/publisher and the reader. And when you're self-publishing, you're taking a book straight to the reader, so you need to consider carefully what the reader is looking for.

As a basis, a reader wants a book that is:

- Following genre conventions: An erotic novel had better have some steamy scenes; a book entitled *How to Unblock a U-bend* had better show the reader exactly how to unblock a U-bend, not just waffle on about the history of U-bends. A reader wants to pick a book up knowing, to a degree, what to expect.
- Professionally presented: Whether you've self-published or been published traditionally, the book needs to have a decent cover, a good blurb, quality printing and no daft typos.
- Sensibly priced: Twenty-five quid for a cookbook? Forget it.
- Well-written: The author needs to have a mastery of

language and the writing must be clear, flowing, well-structured, consistent and accurate.

For non-fiction, a book must:
- Inform.
- Be accurate.
- Present the right content in the right order.
- Be based on a credible, educated opinion.

For fiction, a book must be compelling and intriguing, and it may also be:
- A work of art
- Beautiful
- Clever
- Educative
- Exciting
- Moving
- Thought-provoking

Most of all, a reader wants to feel comfortable that you, the author, know what you're doing in writing a book. I assess many books that come through The Book Specialist. And the best, by far, are those where I'm relaxed as I read because I have the sense that the author is in charge and really knows where he's taking me and how. These are the books that I start to read and can't put down; although I only intended to read the first couple of chapters, before I know it my husband's shouting that dinner's ready and I've spent the afternoon lost in the book.

MB example: *The Hunger Games* by Suzanne Collins

I go into my local bookshop for a browse and I pick up *The Hunger Games*. It's lying on a table in the young adult section, next to books by Stephenie Meyer, Cassandra Clare, Maggie Stiefvater and Rick Riordan and lots of other young adult novels. The cover is interesting, and clearly very well designed – and it fits with the genre. I pick the book up; great, it's not too thin, not too fat. I turn it over and read the back blurb: looks interesting. I check the price: £7.99, the usual price I'd expect to see. I flick through the pages: font looks about right, and pages and print are of a decent quality. I read the first paragraph; I like the writing style, the writer can clearly write and I want to read on. I take the book to the counter and buy it.

Being a Marketable Author

Writing a marketable book isn't enough – you also need to be a marketable author.

Once upon a time you could be a total recluse, hidden away from the world, invisible to the public, and have a successful career as an author. Those days are gone. Books have to be marketed, and marketing involves the author being known to the reader.

The business of publishing has evolved, and society has developed a fascination with all things celebrity – and an expectation that anyone putting out a creative work for sale will be public-facing. If you've written a non-fiction book, you'll need to be generating publicity in the field to drive sales – speaking at events, perhaps, or penning articles for a trade magazine. If you're a novelist and you want to sell lots of books, you've got to expect readers to be interested in you, the author, so you write a blog and tweet and do book signings and so on.

Many authors find this side of publishing abhorrent – they just want to quietly write a book, thank you very much, and get on with their life without getting sucked into the razzmatazz. Completely understandable. But not ideal for putting out a marketable book.

Think about what an agent or publisher is looking for in an author:

- Friendly
- Good with people
- Happy to help
- Happy to take guidance
- Intelligent
- Professional (see Chapter 1)
- Respectful

Remember: An agent/publisher is looking for an author who understands that he must be easy to work with and marketable to readers.

UMB examples: The unmarketable author

- You refuse to take part in any marketing activities.

- You refuse to follow guidance or instructions.
- You row with and/or publicly slate your agent.
- You row with and/or publicly slate your publisher.
- You row with and/or publicly slate readers.
- You row with and/or publicly slate other authors.
- You expect your agent/publisher to baby you/worship you/be at your beck and call.
- You don't bother to respond to emails/calls from your agent, publisher and/or readers.

Beyond having a good understanding of the business of publishing and the right attitude, authors are marketable when they have:

- Already published successfully: You've got a book or several books under your belt.
- An interesting background: You're a direct descendant of Charles Dickens and you write a modern-day version of *Oliver Twist*. You were held hostage by monkeys in a South American jungle and you write about your experiences. You're ten years old and you write an astonishingly beautiful adult novel.
- Established a readership already: Perhaps you hold three world championship titles for tiddlywinks and you're famous and intriguing to the 50,000 members of the Tiddlywinks Association – there's your market for a book on your journey to success, or a guide to world-class tiddlywinking.
- Expertise in their field: You're a psychologist, and you write a book on overcoming anxiety. You're a historian and a founder of the Museum of Toys, and you write a book about the history of toys. You're a police detective

superintendent, and you write a crime thriller.

- Good contacts for publicity: Your best friend is the editor of the *Guardian*. Richard and Judy owe you a favour. You've already been on BBC News, Radio One and Radio Five Live. Your next-door neighbour is Kate Mosse (with an 'e'; Kate Moss won't be much help).
- Relevant writing experience: You're a journalist, or a professional copywriter. You've won a national short story competition. You've had a poem published in an anthology. You've written an article for the *Sunday Times*. You've a master's degree in creative writing.

It is possible to get published or to self-publish successfully without ticking any of these boxes. But the more extras you have, the easier marketing becomes.

Toolkit: Identify what makes you a marketable author. Jot down your answers in your toolkit.

For more on marketing yourself as an author, take a look at Chapter 17.

In a Nutshell

- A marketable book has a market and pleases that market.
- You need to care about marketability if you want to sell books.
- Know your competition: what will make your book stand out in the crowd?
- Understand how literary agents operate, and what they're looking for.

- Understand how publishers operate, and what they're looking for.
- Know what readers want.
- Think about how you, as author, are marketable.

3. Coming Up with the Big Idea

So you've had an idea for a book. With mounting excitement, you fire up your laptop, open a new document, save it as 'The Book', take a deep breath and start typing.

Woah there!

If you want to write a decent book, a marketable book, then before you start writing there's a good deal of groundwork to be done.

The more thinking about the idea you do before writing, the better your book will be. Fact. The best books I've read and edited over the years have been carefully conceived. The worst books have quite clearly been bashed out without any solid foundations.

The idea is everything. A beautifully written and widely marketed book based on a poor idea will not do well. A book that has grown out of a great idea; now that's one people want to read.

Generating Ideas

Some writers, myself included, spend their days fighting ideas off with a stick. We're bombarded at every turn with ideas (most of them going nowhere), and it can be a pretty exhausting business. I've lost track of the number of times I've said excitedly to my husband, 'I've had an idea for a book!'

These days he gives a long-suffering sigh and trudges off to put the kettle on.

But not all writers are full of ideas: inspiration can be elusive, especially for writers who are yet to finish their first book.

If you really want to write a book, but you can't quite pin down an idea, here are some ideas to try:

- Look within. 'Write about what you know' is advice commonly given to wannabe authors. Think about experiences you've had, lessons you've learnt, skills you've developed. Is there a book in them?
- Get out and about, and do some people-watching. Fiction is about people – so the more time you spend watching people, the more ideas emerge.
- Think about what makes you want to write. Is there a place or a song or a picture or a person that most makes you want to write? Explore the connection; perhaps this is the seed of a book.
- Write something, anything. The idea of writing a book – thousands and thousands of words – is daunting. Start small. Write a poem or a short story. Or even just a paragraph. The more often you write, the more your mind will start thinking in terms of writing.
- Explore other art forms. All forms of creative expression inspire. When words won't come, try visual and aural stimulation. A painting, a sculpture, a piece of music, a play, a film – all can fire up the imagination.
- Chat with a friend. If you know someone who's a bookworm and/or a writer, talk books with that person.

Brainstorm together. You may even find that a co-writing project grows out of such an activity.

- Look back through history. Read biographies, read historical non-fiction books. A story from the past can spark an idea.
- Get in the habit of making notes. Keep a notebook with you at all times, and scribble thoughts down as they come to you. Sometimes a great idea comes when you're not expecting it and is fleeting – catch it quickly.
- Read and read and read, and then read some more. The absolute best way to generate ideas is to read books. Lots of books. Don't limit yourself to reading books within your favourite genre(s); push yourself to read beyond your established taste. Read fantasy and sci-fi and literary fiction and chicklit. Read picture books and Manga. Read how-to guides and travelogues and biographies. Not only will you discover new books you enjoy and broaden your understanding of subjects and of writing styles, but you'll hone what kind of book you want to write. And don't just read books – read blogs, websites, magazines, newspapers.

The best way to open yourself to ideas is to start by turning off the part of you that judges ideas. Let all ideas come. Give them a chance. Something you start off thinking is bonkers may actually turn out to be an exciting, interesting idea.

Chasing a Trend

One way to write a marketable book is to look very carefully at trends in publishing and try to jump on board. So if you notice that techno-thrillers are all the rage, you write a techno-thriller.

If this is your strategy then I commend you for your businesslike approach to writing a book; but do be aware that trends come and go pretty quickly. In the time it takes you to write your book, publishing may be onto the next fad. This is particularly important to note if you want to take your book to an agent/publisher. The books you're seeing in the bookshops at the moment took a year or more to get from the agents' desks to the shelves. So by now agents and publishers are looking for something new and fresh.

If you do want to write a trendy book, go for it – but please make sure that your idea is sufficiently original to pass muster. See the later section 'Checking That Your Idea Is Original'.

Try This: Start reading *The Bookseller*, the UK publishing industry's trade magazine. Each week you'll see what the trends are, and – crucially – what people are buying.

MB example: *Knit Your Own Royal Wedding* by Fiona Goble

Fiona Goble spotted an emerging trend – public interest in the forthcoming royal wedding – and jumped on board; and so did her publisher, Ivy Press. Her fun book got good reviews and coverage in the media, and sold well among the other books chasing the trend like Ladybird's *William and Kate: The Royal Wedding*, Sunbird's *Royal Wedding: Dress-Up Dolly Book* and Simon & Schuster's *Will and Kate's Big Fat Gypsy Wedding*.

Coming up with a Book Series

Book series are marketable. Readers like big, intricate stories. They like enjoying one book and realising that there are another two or more to read yet. They like being left in suspense after Book 1, and chomping at the bit to read Book 2. They like authors who are clever enough and controlled enough in their writing to make a story really last.

Your book series could be:

- A non-fiction series on a theme: For example, *The 4-Hour Work Week* and *The 4-Hour Body* by Timothy Ferriss (and no doubt there will be more titles to follow soon; I'm hoping for *The 4-Hour Book Writer*).
- A chronological story with the same character as protagonist, split into chunks: For example, Becca Fitzpatrick's books *Hush, Hush*, *Crescendo* and *Silence* form three parts of a story.
- A series of separate stories with the same character as protagonist, all of which tie into an overarching story: For example, Patricia Cornwell's Dr Kay Scarpetta novels – each is a standalone story, but there's overarching character and plot development.
- A series of separate stories that include the same set of characters, but have different protagonists: For example, Penny Avis and Joanna Berry's four-book *Never Mind the Botox* series, which covers the same event as experienced by four professional women, each book told from a different character's point of view.

When considering a series, keep in mind that you must be able to sustain the reader's interest over all the books – the plot and characters must be sufficiently intriguing to make a reader want to read on. And each book must stand alone as a cohesive whole with a sound start, middle and end. A reader must be able to dive into a series at Book 3 and pick up the story. And the reader mustn't be frustrated at the end of Book 1 because you've just cut the story off without any sense of closure.

MB example: *The Chronicles of Narnia* by CS Lewis

A classic bestselling fantasy series. The story spans seven books, each of which effectively stands alone but is tied to all the others through plot, characters and setting. The final book – *The Last Battle* – draws the overarching story to a satisfying close. Interestingly, Lewis did not write the books in chronological order. For example, Book 1 – *The Magician's Nephew* – was written last.

When it comes to book series, three is a magic number. Unless your idea is exceptionally good, and makes for a sustainable, long, complex plot, don't attempt a ten-book series for your first foray into fiction.

Really Exploring Your Idea

Inspiration strikes, adrenalin rushes through you: you've had an idea and you want to write and write and write.

Ideas often come with a whole burst of energy, and there's a sense of panic – if you don't get this down, fast, you may lose it. My advice: keep a notebook handy, and write down everything that comes into your mind. Then step back and take some time to let the idea grow and develop and, finally, settle.

Great ideas are the ones that linger for days, haunting you. They're the ones that you just can't shake off, that stalk you in your dreams.

Give yourself the time and space to explore the idea. Don't think about the nitty gritty of writing the book for now; just sit with the idea and see what comes. Keep writing down everything that comes into your mind, even if you want to instantly dismiss it. Later, you may be interested in a thought that once seemed irrelevant or silly.

This is the fun bit of writing a book, so enjoy it. Don't rush into writing, or planning to write. Until you get to a point where the idea has settled and is unchanging, just roll with the creative process.

Checking That Your Idea Is Good

You've got an idea, and you're excited about it. You'd love to have this book on your shelf. The question is: will anyone else?

If you're just writing for yourself, you can run with any idea you've settled on. But if you're writing a book that you want others to read, enjoy and recommend to their friends, you need to be sure that the readers will agree that your idea is good.

Your idea may be great if it's:
- Clever – it makes the reader think.
- Educative – the reader learns something by reading it.
- Emotionally affective – it moves the reader.
- Exciting – it's a brilliant, addictive read.
- Funny – it makes the reader smile.
- Intriguing – it makes the reader want to read on.
- Original – it takes the reader somewhere brand new.
- Powerful – it changes the reader.

Conversely, your idea may be one to give up on if it's:
- Boring – not a lot happens; the idea isn't enthralling.
- Lame – it's trying to be amusing or clever, and failing miserably.
- Offensive – it's racist or sexist or any other –*ist*.
- Preaching – it's bossy and prescriptive.
- Silly – it's about a man who turns into a roller-skating hamster.
- Unbelievable – it's about Prince Harry marrying Susan Boyle.
- Unoriginal – the reader's read it all before.

So how can you tell whether your idea is a keeper? Here are some ideas:
- Take plenty of time to consider it. I often have a blindingly brilliant idea for a book on my way to bed. The next morning, after a decent sleep, I realise it's actually a blindingly bad idea. That's simply how it works with ideas!
- Be your own critic. In the 'Generating Ideas' section,

earlier in this chapter, I encouraged you to turn off your judgement and give ideas a chance. Now's the time to get tough with yourself – is this idea good?

- Run it by friends and family. Take on board their opinions: you don't have to agree with any of them, but all feedback helps you crystallise your thinking.

- Talk with your target readers. If your idea is for a business book, talk to your colleagues. If you want to write a book for dentists, talk to dentists. If you've an idea for a young adult novel, run it by some teenagers.

- Ask a professional. If you're really serious about your book, ask a professional editor/writer to assess the idea. Some offer a mentoring service where you can pay for an hour or so of an editor's time during which you brainstorm the idea together.

'But what about confidentiality?' I hear you ask. Your idea is precious to you, of course, and you may worry about sharing it with others in case they steal it. Anything you *write* is protected by copyright law, but *ideas* are not. In truth, writing a book is a huge undertaking, and there are very few people out there dedicated, equipped and unscrupulous enough to take your idea, write a book and beat you to publishing it. But perhaps don't do the rounds of writers' groups telling everyone you meet about your idea. And if you're really anxious about sharing your idea, work with a professional editor with whom confidentiality is assured.

> # MB example: *Before I Go to Sleep* by SJ Watson
>
> A bestselling book that's earned some impressive reviews: 'Quite simply the best debut I've ever read' (Tess Gerritsen); 'a superior literary page-turner' (*Sunday Times*); 'an absolute cracker… faultless' (*Daily Mail*); 'exceptionally accomplished' (*Guardian*). 'Its set-up is brilliantly simple,' writes Adrian Turpin for the *Financial Times*. And that's really the heart of the book's success. It's very well-written, especially in the structuring, and the characters are intriguing – but it's the simple idea at the core of the book that makes it a success. If you've read *Before I Go to Sleep*, you'll know what I mean. If you haven't, go get a copy!

Checking That You're the Right Person to Write the Book

So you've had an idea for a novel for children aged five to seven. Do you have children? Nieces and nephews? Grandchildren? Are you a primary school teacher? A boys' footie coach? No? Are you sure you have enough current experience with children to write for children?

Say your idea is for a thriller set in an underground world of S&M – a top-shelf kind of book. Do you know about S&M? Or are you more of an M&S type? A hot and steamy thriller is no good if the filthiest word in the book is *appendage*.

Perhaps you want to write a book about living with diabetes. Are you a doctor? A nutritionist? A diabetic, even? Nope? You're going to struggle to convince the reader that you're a credible author for this book.

As I explain in Chapter 2, you need to be a marketable author for the book you're writing. Make sure that the book idea and you as author marry up.

Checking That Your Idea Is Original

Before you spend the next year buried in your novel, be sure that you're creating something, well, novel.

Your first job, once you've got a concrete idea for a book that you think is pretty decent and fits you as author, is to get yourself on Amazon (www.amazon.co.uk) and spend a couple of hours carefully researching whether it's been done before.

With any luck, you find that your idea really does have legs. But don't be too disheartened if you find, instead, that the idea's not a goer, because:

- Another author had the same idea, and beat you to it. Say you want to write a book that brings together the experiences of your favourite football club's supporters. You've never seen a book like it, and all your mates say it sounds great. But then you look online and discover that such a book already exists, or is soon to publish. Darn it.

- You've blatantly copied another author. You love the *Twilight* series, and you want to write a romance about a vampire called Edmund, a werewolf called Jack and a girl called Belle, set in a town called Knives, in which baddie vampires go after Belle. Sounds a lot like a *Twilight* copy to me.

- You've unconsciously copied another author. You've had

this great idea for a book, and you can't remember anyone doing it before. It's a thriller in which dinosaurs are brought back to life and they escape, causing havoc. Two words for you: *Jurassic Park*.

Of course, your idea doesn't have to be breathtakingly new (see the following section, 'Checking the Market'). Just take a look at the surge of paranormal vampire fiction published in the wake of *Twilight*. Most writers take inspiration from other books. But the key is not to be a copycat. You need a new take on a tale, a fresh angle, an exciting approach.

MB example: *Harry Potter* by JK Rowling

In 2011, a US judge dismissed a £500 million plagiarism lawsuit against JK Rowling. The estate of late author Adrian Jacobs claimed that Rowling had lifted plot aspects in *Harry Potter and the Goblet of Fire* from Jacobs' 1987 children's book, *The Adventures of Willy the Wizard No 1: Livid Land*. Rowling claimed she'd never read *Willy the Wizard*, and the US judge stated, 'The contrast between the total concept and feel of the works is so stark that any serious comparison of the two strains credulity.' The bottom line: Rowling's book was sufficiently original.

Checking the Market

You've worked out that your idea is original; it hasn't been done before. Now you need to decide whether a market exists for your book. Unless you already have readers lined up to read your book – you're a celebrity, say, or a hugely successful entrepreneur – you're going to need to check that people will want to read your book.

There are three questions you need to consider.

In What Genre Does the Book Fit?

Some authors get hot and bothered about genres. 'Why must I pigeon-hole my book?' is a question I hear frequently. Because if your book is to be marketable, it needs to have a clear place in the market – it needs to slot into a genre.

A *genre* is a category that helps:

- You or a publisher know how to market the book: The genre informs the marketing strategy. For example, for a women's fiction book, you may pitch articles to women's magazines and offer a spa mini-break competition to entice readers to a website that sells the book. For a non-fiction business book, you may look to business networking organisations and conferences for promotional possibilities.
- Book retailers know in what section to place your book. There's not much point publishing a funny autobiography entitled *Eating My Heart Out* if it ends up shelved with the cookery books.
- Readers know what to expect from your book. Hugely important. There are millions of books in the world, and the reader needs some means of narrowing down the choice. Genres allow readers to decide what kind of book

they want to read – from a weighty tome on rock formation to a whodunnit.

Many different genres exist. Here's a by-no-means-exhaustive list:

- Fiction: Action and adventure, children's, commercial fiction, crime, erotica, fantasy, historical fiction, literary fiction, mystery, picture books, paranormal, sci-fi, romance, thriller, young adult, women's fiction.
- Non-fiction: Art, auto-/biography, business, cookery and food, film and TV, gardening, health and fitness, history, humour and gift, finance, lifestyle, MBS (mind, body and spirit), music, psychology, reference, relationships, religion, self-help, science and technology, sports, travel.

Within those genres you have sub-genres and crossovers, such as paranormal romance, erotic fantasy and cyberpunk sci-fi.

Try This: Don't get yourself in knots working out genres. Go to your local bookshop and see how the books are categorised.

Some novels are genre-benders – it's hard to know quite where they fit. For your first book, when you want to ensure good marketability, I advise sticking to writing within an established genre.

UMB example: The how-many-genres-can-I-incorporate approach

It's a children's book but you think adults will love it too. It's a crime thriller set in the Wild West in which the criminals are werewolves, and aliens run the local saloon, and a man and a woman must find love against the odds, and an old man must come to terms with the loss of his wife, and a professional woman is struggling to find a balance between career and mothering, and a small boy is trying to teach a whole load of cowboys the game of football, and a computer virus is spreading through the community (a time traveller brought PCs to the ranch). Oh, and at the end there's a five-chapter history lesson on cowboys and Native Americans.

CAN YOU SEE A MARKET FOR THE BOOK?

You're writing a book within a genre – whether it's science fiction, autobiography or military history. You need to look at the genre and see what books exist already.

Go on Amazon and browse in your local bookshop. Check out the competition for your book – which books in the genre are similar to yours? For example, if you want to write an autobiography of your experiences as a soldier in Iraq, look at all other autobiographies of soldiers in Iraq, and more recent soldier memoirs too. If you want to write a rhyming, collage-art picture book about zoo animals, look at all picture books about animals and zoos, all collage-art picture books and all rhyming picture books. If you want to write a crime thriller about a detective set in London, look at all the crime thrillers, especially those set in a UK city and with a detective as the protagonist.

You may find that:

• Many books exist that would compete with yours. Hmm,

that's a worry. You've proven that there's a big market for your book – but is yours going to stand out? If all these titles will compete with your book, you're going to struggle to make good sales.

- Some books exist that would compete with yours. Good. The market exists already, but isn't oversaturated. What counts is that your book will sit nicely alongside these titles, but have an edge (see the following section 'How Will Your Book Stand Out in the Market?').

- No book on earth would compete with yours. Authors commonly think this is good news. I generally don't. If your book idea is groundbreakingly new to the point where nothing within its genre remotely comes close, you're either a genius (possible, but unlikely) or your book idea hasn't been done before for the simple reason that it's rubbish (see the earlier section 'Checking That Your Idea Is Good').

Remember: Publishers interested in your book will ask you for a list of competing titles. What do they want to see? Some competing titles! They don't want a 40-page list of books. They don't want a blank page. They want a handful of books that show a market exists… and then they want to see how your book will stand out (see the following section).

Sometimes, you identify a gap in the market. Be careful: this shouldn't mean that no book on earth would compete with yours; what it means is that you can pull together threads of books already published to offer something new.

> ## MB example: *How to Succeed as a Freelancer in Publishing* by Charlie Wilson and Emma Murray
>
> *How to Succeed as a Freelancer in Publishing* stepped out into new territory. Emma and I knew that a market existed for a book on freelancing in publishing: we'd been bombarded with questions from freelancers for years, and were well-connected in the freelancing community. When we came to research writing a book on the subject, we quickly realised that no such book existed. There were books on publishing. There were books on freelancing. There were no books on freelancing in publishing. Our book was picked up by a publisher because it filled a gap in a market that clearly existed.

Word to the Wise: Tread carefully with an autobiography. The so-called 'misery memoir' genre is already full of many harrowing accounts of difficult personal experiences, such as child abuse. In fact, it's become difficult to convince a publisher that there's a market for a memoir of someone not already known to the public unless the story is really, really, really terrible. Sensational. Deeply shocking.

How Will Your Book Stand Out in the Market?

Having established that some competing titles exist, you need to think about what will make your book stand out in the market. What makes it different, special, worth reading?

In marketing-speak, what you're looking for is a USP – a

unique selling point. You should be able to sum this up in a sentence or two.

- *The only book on the new sensation, naked hang-gliding.*
- *The only book about the exciting new branch of physics, subatromicpartafusionnuclearism.*
- *A 21st-century retelling of Snow White set against the backdrop of the Arab Spring uprising.*
- *A family drama told from the perspective of an autistic child.*

USPs for non-fiction are quite easy – you find an unexplored angle. For example, I wrote a book about parenting (*Survival Guide for New Parents: Pregnancy, Birth and the First Year*). There are many, many books on parenting. But I noticed that most of them were pretty bossy; that few covered the span from conception to the first birthday; and that none, in my opinion, successfully focused on the parent's experience. From the wealth of books available on parenting, I could see that a market existed for books on the subject, but I set my book apart from the others.

Novels are trickier, but you should still be able to come up with a line that describes the essence of the story and looks sufficiently different to competing titles. If you're struggling, browse through blurbs (the copy that goes on the back cover and 'sells' the book) online and in bookshops. Start to get a feel for what publishers draw out as making a book worth reading. Then have a go at writing your own blurb for your idea. What do you think – does it fit into the genre but also stand out as being novel and interesting?

MB example: *French Women Don't Get Fat* by Mireille Guiliano

From the back cover blurb: 'How *do* French women do it? This is the book that unlocks the simple secrets of "the French paradox" – how to enjoy food and stay slim and healthy.' A neat, comprehensive, clear USP. No wonder the book is an international bestseller.

The Final Idea

Having worked your way through the preceding sections in this chapter, you now have a choice:

- Put your idea aside.
- Make your idea into a book.

PUTTING THE IDEA ASIDE

If you've explored your idea and you just don't have confidence that it will lead to a marketable book, you're best putting that idea aside for now. The vast majority of ideas don't go anywhere. It's a shame when you've been excited about an idea, but far better to let it go and move on to something better than write a book that doesn't come up to scratch.

Remember: I'm not telling you to *abandon* your idea entirely, but to put it aside for now. Gather up all the notes you made and put them in an 'Ideas' folder that you keep somewhere safe. Keeping all your ideas is worthwhile because:

- In doing so you are valuing the idea you created, which means you're more likely to come up with more ideas.
- Over time you see how you are developing as a writer, as your ideas improve.
- You never know, you may use that idea in the future. You may come up with a way to develop it, or you may weave part of it into a different idea, or you may reach a point where you decide that the book you thought of is now marketable, whereas it wasn't ten years ago when you conceived the idea.

DECIDING TO WRITE THE BOOK

Hopefully, you've got to this point in the chapter and decided that your idea is great, and that your book will be marketable. Hooray! You've thoroughly explored the idea, and can now have confidence as you move forward in the process.

You've done a lot of very valuable work thinking about the marketability of your book. Don't sail off now and forget all you've learnt – set it down so you can refer to it from here on.

Toolkit: Write down the following:
- The book's title, if you have any idea of this yet (head to Chapters 5 and 8 for more on the title)
- The genre of your book
- The key competing titles for your book

- Your book's USP

Keep that toolkit close; you'll be using it often.

Your next step: preparing to write. Turn to Chapter 4 for details.

In a Nutshell

- If you need inspiration, get out and about and drink in the world.
- Carry a notebook with you, and scribble down thoughts.
- When it comes to ideas, be open-minded.
- Keep up-to-date with trends in publishing.
- Give an idea space and time to develop.
- Carefully consider whether your idea is a good one.
- Ask others for their opinions.
- Make sure your idea is novel.
- Determine how much competition your book would face.
- Check that you have a USP (unique selling point).
- If the idea's not working, put it aside – but keep it safe.
- If you're happy that the idea is good, prepare to write.

4. Preparing to Write

Preparation is boring, I know. It's much more fun writing a book than planning to write a book. But take off your *artiste* hat for a little while and don your serious, professional author one. Working through the contents of this chapter needn't take you long, and the results will greatly improve the marketability of your book.

Knowing the Benefits of Planning

As an author mentor, I've helped many authors plan their book before they put pen to paper or finger to keyboard. And I've seen, time and time again, how a little effort at the start of the process pays off over the course of writing the book. Here are the key benefits of planning before writing:

- The final book is focused. By working out the theme, the angle and the point of the book clearly before you write, you create a book whose focus is crystal clear. And readers like focused books. So do publishers. So do retailers.

- The final book is well organised. Readers need to have the sense that the author knows where the book is going at all points. As a reader, nothing infuriates me more than a book that's meandering about vaguely with no sense of structure. In the books I edit, poor structuring is a common issue – straightforward planning before writing prevents this problem.

- The final book is thorough. All angles have been considered. There are no holes in the plot, no topics forgotten. If you've written a guide to plumbing for home-owners, you haven't neglected to mention unblocking a sink. If you've written a novel set in Brighton, you haven't forgotten to mention Brighton.

- The final book fits into its genre. You've studied the genre in which you're writing, and you're following its conventions. So your horror novel does actually have some grisly events in it, and your picture book has pictures. (Sounds obvious? You'd be amazed how many books I've come across that don't follow genre conventions.)

- You write confidently. Once you've planned your book, you know exactly what you're doing – so there's no bumbling about in the dark, no worrying that the final book will be a complete disaster.

- You save yourself time and effort. Many of the problems that I see in books can be avoided by careful planning. Sorting problems out after the book is written is hard work, and often involves extensive rewriting.

Hopefully, I've convinced you of the need to plan. The following sections take you through all the prep you need to carry out before you can begin writing.

Starting as You Mean to Go On: Carefully

Before diving into preparing your book, it's worth giving a little thought to how carefully you're working.

By far the biggest mistake I see authors make is rushing their writing. I've had authors send books to The Book Specialist who quite clearly have hammered away at their computers without ever reading back a single sentence they've written. 'I wrote this novel in a fortnight!' they boast. I've yet to see a book written in such a cavalier fashion be any good.

Of course, this is an extreme, and most authors who rush don't take it quite that far. But still I see plenty of writing that clearly hasn't been carefully thought out and toiled over. And the bottom line is that unless you're an exceptional writer, you're unlikely to get away with bashing out a book. Creating a book is a marathon, not a sprint.

There are various reasons why you may be slapdash in writing your book:

- You want to finish before you run out of steam. When a book is flooding out of you, it's fabulous – you're inspired, the muse is with you, everything just slots into place. But life often gets in the way. You have a family, friends, a job. You have to do inconvenient things like eat and sleep and wash. The writing process is constantly interrupted. You worry that you'll lose your mojo. So you churn out the book as fast as you can. The result: a book that reads like it's been churned out fast.

- You don't particularly enjoy the writing process and you want to get it out of the way. Perhaps you're more interested in being a published author than the actual process of writing. For example, the book you're writing may simply be a tool for marketing yourself or your business. If you can't be bothered to write the book well, don't write it. No book is better than a poor book. Alternatively, if your funds can stretch that far, hire a ghostwriter.

- You don't realise that you write better when you take your time. Try it one day. Choose a topic and write on it for ten minutes. Then choose another topic and write on it for an hour. See the difference in your writing.

- You want to publish quickly. This is a key factor for many authors. They spot a trend, and they want to chase it. Especially popular at the moment is publishing in ebook format through Amazon for the Kindle. There have been some impressive success stories of people doing so – and many authors are following suit, knocking out novels in the hope of making big bucks. You may be lucky enough to make a mint putting out a shoddy, rushed book (indeed, some of those who've sold very well on Amazon haven't written great books). But you're more likely to see disappointing results and damage your potential to be a prolific, professional author who's taken seriously. For more on trend-chasing, see Chapter 3.

Don't misunderstand the point of this section. I'm not saying you can't write fast if that's how you write most easily. But just because you can write a chapter in an hour, doesn't mean that chapter is then finished and ready to publish! Write quickly by all means, but write carefully – go back over your writing

again and again until you've got it as good as it can be. For
more on editing your writing, go to Chapter 15.

Getting to Know the Genre

In Chapter 2, I look at identifying the genre into which your
book fits. Armed with that knowledge, you now need to read
plenty of books within the genre. How many? As many as you
can possibly manage.

At this stage, you need to move beyond reading as you've
always done – for the sheer pleasure of it – and start reading
critically. Read as a writer. Look carefully at all aspects of the
book, and use what you learn to develop your own writing.

Here are some questions to consider when reading books in
the genre:

- What do you think of the title?
- What do you think of the blurb (the back-cover copy)?
- How does the book meet the key conventions of this
  genre?
- Does the book pull away from the genre conventions at
  all? How does that work out?
- What is the language like?
- For fiction books: How much dialogue is there? How
  much description? Do you like the characters? Do you
  like the plot? What about the setting?
- For non-fiction books: Is the book serving its purpose? Is
  it clear and engaging? Is it adequately exploring the
  subject matter?

- How long is the book?
- How long are chapters?
- How is the book structured?
- What is the author voice like?
- How does the book you're planning to write sit against this book? Is it better? Is it too similar?
- Do you like the book? Why?
- What are the book's strengths?
- What are the book's weaknesses?

Also note the publisher of the book, whether it's self-published or traditionally published, and the price, and take a look at any marketing materials for the book and the author, such as a website.

Look at book reviews too: in newspapers, in magazines, on websites and – crucially – on book bloggers' sites. When you finish reading a book, Google it and read what others are saying about it. Consider whether you agree with the opinions. Try to identify why a book is doing well, and why another one isn't.

Finally, engage with other materials within the genre. For example, if you're writing a science-fiction book, watch sci-fi films and TV shows. If you're reading *Harry Potter*, watch the movies.

Remember: Keep your brain in gear. Don't just take in information passively; really think. Learn what makes a good book by looking around you.

Getting to Know Your Reader

Who exactly is your reader? This is a question a publisher will ask, and even if you intend to self-publish, it's one you must ask yourself too. Think of it this way: if you don't know who the reader is, you can't market the book successfully to that reader.

In the world of business, marketing professionals segment a market by various factors, which helps them identify the people to target in their marketing campaigns. They conduct market research, and come up with a profile of their customers. For example, at the time of writing research indicates that in the UK most e-reader devices are owned by women aged between 45 and 54. So these women are key readers for ebooks.

When considering who'll read your book, think about the reader's:

- Age
- Gender
- Interests
- Occupation
- Socio-economic status

You soon start to build up a picture of the kind of reader you expect to like your book.

Of course, the broader the market, the broader the scope for selling the book. Knowing this, many authors deliberately try to write for a very wide readership. I've had authors tell me that their books are 'for anyone from age ten to a hundred'. That's a very wide range! Do ten-year-olds really read the same books as pensioners? It's better to be realistic about the readers you're writing for at the outset – a book with a clear, focused market does better than a book that's trying to appeal to everyone.

Word to the Wise: Don't take forming a picture of the reader too far. You don't want to end up writing a book purely for Dame Doris, age 59, who's super-posh and lives in Dorset in a stately home, when actually your book would also appeal to Sandra, age 40, who's a checkout assistant and lives in a council flat in Manchester. Be as inclusive as you can when working out your target readership – just be realistic as you do so.

Toolkit: Once you've established the profile of your target reader, add it to your toolkit.

What if you haven't the foggiest who reads the kind of book you want to write? Well, that's rather worrying at this stage – especially when you've got to know the genre (see the previous section). Are you certain you're cut out to write in this genre if you're not really sure who reads the books? Yes? Okay, well get online and start doing more reading about the genre – see who's chatting about these books online. Be a detective, and ferret out who's reading what. (Goodreads.com is an excellent starting point.)

Researching

Some books require no research. For example, you may be

writing a fantasy novel set in the year 2330. Or you may be writing an autobiography, and have all the information you need in your mind.

Other books require some legwork. If you're writing a novel about a man who's haunted by his experiences flying a Spitfire in World War II, you'd better have a good understanding of World War II and of pilots and planes during this era. If you're writing a guide to buying a house, you'd better be clued up on the ins and outs of house-buying – laws, procedures, parties involved and so on.

Knowing How Much Research To Do

The worst thing you can do is skimp on research if your book requires it. A reader is quick to spot a lazy writer.

That said, there's a balance between researching well and researching in ridiculous detail. Say two paragraphs of a chapter are devoted to a character catching a train from London to Edinburgh. By all means check which station he would leave from, at which he would arrive and the total journey time if you need these details in the plot. But don't feel the need to get on a train in London and go up to Edinburgh just so you can travel in your character's shoes.

Word to the Wise: If you've done lots of research for your book, that's great. But don't shove it down the reader's throat. This isn't an essay at school, where you get points for impressing the teacher with how much research you carried out. This is a book. Only what's essential should be in there.

Using Different Methods to Research

So how do you go about researching? Here are some avenues you can explore:

- Head to your local library. Remember that building with all the lovely books that the Government's threatening to close? Make use of it! You'll find loads of books of interest, and if you talk to librarians, you'll find they're mines of information.

- Read books on the subject. If your book is about architecture, read other books about architecture. If your novel is set in a French vineyard, read non-fiction titles on wine-growing in France.

- Look at images. Don't just rely on words; check out pictures too. A Google Images search for a keyword brings up lots of images that can inform your writing, especially descriptions of places and people and things. Stick inspiring photos up on the wall of your writing space.

- Surf the net. The internet is your best tool for research. Do bear in mind, however, that not all web sources are equal when it comes to credibility.

- Talk to experts in the field. If a character in your book has a brain tumour, try to track down a neurosurgeon.

- Visit places if they're important in the book. If you're writing a history of the Science Museum in London, go there. If you're writing a biography of Charlotte Brontë, head to Yorkshire.

Toolkit: Keep a research file, where you collate notes, printouts, photocopies and pictures.

ENSURING FACTUAL ACCURACY

Mistakes in your content are completely unforgiveable. Do your research thoroughly, and double-check facts. Don't:

- Trust Wikipedia.
- Guess.
- Exaggerate.
- Make stuff up.

Take special care with research if the details of your book are potentially sensational. For example, if you're writing an exposé that's going to send the media into a frenzy and capture the public's attention, be absolutely sure that you have your facts correct.

> # MB example: *The Da Vinci Code* by Dan Brown
>
> Brown's 2003 novel is undoubtedly a marketable book, having sold many millions of copies worldwide and made Brown a whole heap of money. A book that overturned commonly held beliefs about Christian history was always going to ruffle feathers, but it's concerning how many historians claim that Brown's book contains inaccuracies. As an example, Brown writes that the Dead Sea Scrolls were found in the 1950s; in fact, they were found in 1947. What Brown presents as fact is, according to many experts,

> a twisted version of the truth – fiction. Brown was lucky that his book was marketable *despite* issues with the facts. Don't follow in his footsteps; make your book marketable *because* the facts are sound.

Here are some tips for ensuring the quality of your information:

- Only use reputable sources. For example, in this book I've used figures from Neilson BookScan, the publishing industry's sales analysis service. I wouldn't, however, assume that a statistic on a book blogger's website is correct without checking the source.

- Ask an expert in the field to check the veracity of your book. Top publishers hire technical editors to check books whose content a copy editor can't adequately assess. For example, if you're a scientist and have written a book on the origins of the universe, a publisher may bring in a peer reviewer to check your facts.

- If your budget can stretch, hire a professional researcher to fact-check. Check the person's credentials carefully – you need someone experienced whose results you can trust.

Writing the Synopsis

A *synopsis* is an outline of your book – if it's a novel, it's a short summary of the story; if it's a non-fiction book, it's a summary of the content. The synopsis explains the essence of the book.

Authors who intend to seek a publisher for their book are

familiar with the synopsis, because it's a requirement when submitting to publishers and agents. Usually, I find that authors leave writing the synopsis until *after* they've written the book. And then they struggle hugely. In fact, I think this is backwards. You should write the synopsis first, because doing so focuses your writing. If you can't say what your book is about before you write it, how is that book going to be any good? You haven't a clue where it's going.

Even if you intend to self-publish, it's well worth writing a synopsis. It doesn't have to be beautifully crafted at this point: the important thing is to get down the bare bones of the book you intend to write.

Here are some tips for synopsis writing:
- Keep it to one page only. This forces you to summarise.
- Write in the present tense: *It is summer, 1979.*
- Write in the third person, even if your book is in the first person: *John is hit by a car.*
- Don't aim for flowery or blurb-style writing; keep it simple.
- Convey the key themes of the book; for example, redemption, self-discovery.
- Show the reader where the book is set, and when.
- Mention the key characters.
- Outline the key events in the book.
- Show the basic structure – the journey the book takes the reader on.
- Always include the ending. A synopsis is not the place for cliffhangers; you need to know how this story ends!

If you're really struggling to write the synopsis, it may well be because your book is flawed. 'But the plot is just too complex to summarise,' authors tell me. Of course you want your plot to be intricate, but you should still be able to pick out the important events and the key themes. If you can't, it's most likely because you haven't actually yet worked out the core story and its themes. Keep plugging away at it, modifying your book idea as necessary, until you have a one-page summary that really wows.

Try This: If you want to know whether you're on the right lines, show your synopsis to someone who likes reading books in your genre and ask whether this book looks interesting.

Toolkit: Once you're happy with the synopsis, add it to your toolkit.

Writing the One-liner

Now that you've written the synopsis, condense it into a single sentence. 'One sentence!' I hear you cry. 'Impossible!' Essential, actually.

You need to know what your book is in a nutshell. You need to be able to sum it all up in one sentence.

Entrepreneurs talk about the elevator pitch – you get in a lift with a venture capitalist and you have just a minute or so to pitch your amazing business idea to him. You need a similar pitch at the ready. Why? Well, you never know when you'll run into a literary agent! But more importantly, having a one-liner really focuses your writing.

Here's an example of some one-liners:

* *This book is about how to write a book that's got a decent chance of selling.*
* *A book that shows you how to pass your A level history exam.*
* *This is the amazing story of a man who crossed the Sahara Desert on a pogo stick.*
* *The story of a woman with amnesia who's slowly recovering her memory and, in the process, realising her husband isn't her husband at all, but is a psycho.*

Your one-liner is likely to overlap with the USP you came up with in Chapter 3. You may even feel able to combine the two.

Toolkit: Add your one-liner to your toolkit.

Writing the Initial Chapter Breakdown

Chapters 7 and 11 help you with structuring your book. But before you get into the nitty-gritty of structuring, start with a rough chapter breakdown.

Take your synopsis, and flesh it out. Give more detail now, until you've a good idea of the content of the book. Then divide the content into chapters.

Remember: This is a rough outline; a starting point for organising the book. It's likely to change fairly often as you write.

Toolkit: Add the chapter breakdown to your toolkit.

Organising the Job of Writing

You've got a good idea of what you're writing now. But where on earth do you start? Writing an entire book is a daunting task. The page is blank; the Word document is white and the cursor is blinking expectantly.

Break the job down into chunks. Take your chapter breakdown (see the previous section) and use it to map out a framework for writing the book, chapter by chapter.

Here's an example of a writing breakdown:

Chapter	First draft complete	Edited	Proofread
Intro	Y		
1	Y		
2	Y		
3			
4			

A table like this helps you keep track of where you are in your book, and helps you see that you're making progress towards your goal. For non-fiction books, you can set word count targets for each chapter, and then total the word counts to see where you are against your overall target (see Chapter 7). You can see which chapters are complete, which are works in progress and which are yet to be written. You can track the redrafting, review and proofreading stages carefully (though I would advise you don't start these until you've finished a first draft of all chapters). You may also decide to add some deadlines in, to move you forward in the writing.

Toolkit: Pop this writing breakdown table in your author's toolkit.

For fiction, biography and autobiography, I recommend starting at the beginning and writing in a linear fashion. But for non-fiction, dot about as you like.

Try This: Keep each chapter in a separate file until you're happy with it, and then bring all the chapters together at the end. This makes revising and seeing the big picture of the structure easier.

Making Time for Your Writing

I meet a lot of people who tell me they'd love to write a book. 'So what stops you?' I ask them. Sometimes the answer is, 'Oh, I can't write. I'm terrible!' But most often the answer is, 'I dream of doing it, but I never quite get round to it. Life gets in the way. I've no time.'

You'll never write your book unless you make room in your life for writing the book. Don't expect to just write a marketable book by dabbling in writing here and there – a few hundred words one week, a few hundred more five months later. Take your book-writing seriously and give it the time, attention and energy it deserves.

The best approach is to create a writing routine – so you set aside a certain amount of time per day or per week for writing the book. You may write:

- Early in the morning, before your family gets up
- On the train on your way to and from work
- During your lunch hour at work
- Every Saturday morning
- Every evening between seven and nine
- Until silly o'clock on a Friday night

Whatever works for you, go for it – and stick to it.

Toolkit: Write a schedule, and slot it in the folder.

Word to the Wise: Think about how distracted you are in the times you decide to write. You may be a writer who loves tapping away on a laptop in a cafe surrounded by the buzz of other people, and that's fine. But if, instead, you're more of a hermit-in-a-cave kind of writer, make sure the time you designate for writing is time when you can be alone and quiet – not, for example, working on the kitchen table while your children squabble over the toy in the breakfast cereal.

If you're lucky, you may be able to devote a chunk of time to writing at some point; for example, you take a week's holiday from work and spend it writing. Immersing yourself in writing can be very productive, but it's also lonely and tiring, and you feel pressure to write lots and lots. Experiment, and see what works best for you.

Committing to Writing Your Book

You're just about ready to write. Now it's time to make a solid commitment to the book. There's no point coming this far and then struggling to find the time to write, or abandoning the book after a couple of months because you've lost confidence in the idea, or taking ten years to write the book because you can't focus on it. If you're going forward from this point, go all the way.

Decide to write the book, and then do it.

The worst that can happen is that you're not happy with the book you produce, or it turns out that it's not sufficiently marketable because something's gone awry in the ideas, planning and/or writing stages. Your flawed manuscript might be fixable with a bit of professional support. Or you might decide to bin it. Tough, yes, but not the end of the world because you'll have learned heaps during the writing process.

The best that can happen, on the other hand, is that you write a marketable book, it publishes, you market it *and it sells*! You achieve your dream of being a respected, published author whose book is doing well.

Put that way, I hope you'll agree that the potential gain far outweighs the potential pain. So what are you waiting for? Roll up your sleeves, take a deep breath and read on to get into the nitty-gritty of writing your book.

In a Nutshell

- Writing isn't a race. Take your time, and care about quality.

- Be a total know-it-all when it comes to the genre in which you're writing.
- Know who'll read your book.
- If you don't know something for the book, and you ought to know it, do your homework.
- Write a one-page synopsis to overview what you're writing.
- Write a one-line description of the book so that you know the bottom line of what you're writing.
- Write a rough chapter breakdown as a starting point for structuring.
- Break down the writing into manageable chunks.
- Schedule writing time.
- Make a commitment to writing the book, and then get on and do it.

Part 2

What You Write: Non-Fiction

5. Coming Up with a Title

The title of your book is the most important piece of writing you'll do. Every word counts. A good title makes it easy for readers to know what your book's all about and whether they want to read it. A poor title fails to hook the reader – and even if your book is brilliant, it won't sell.

This chapter helps you think about the title you choose for your non-fiction book, looking at different types of title to see what works, and what doesn't.

Word to the Wise: If you're sending your book out to agents/publishers, don't get too attached to the title. Publishers often change titles, with input from their marketing and sales teams.

Toolkit: Add your title to the toolkit.

Golden Rules for Titles

Non-fiction titles must really convey the topic of the book. You want a reader browsing on Amazon to know the point of your book after a quick scan of the title. Follow these pointers when selecting a title:

- Avoid acronyms unless you're sure the reader will know what they stand for.

- Avoid unnecessary jargon.
- Be honest about the book's contents (don't say you offer 1,001 tips when you actually offer 978).
- Check carefully to avoid spelling, punctuation or grammatical errors.
- Convey exactly what the book is about.
- Don't make it too long.
- Don't make overblown claims.
- Don't rip off brands (so don't publish a book called *Cooking with Marmite For Dummies*).
- Ensure that it makes sense.
- Ensure that it's original – check on Amazon that no other book has the same, or a very similar, title.
- Follow conventions (don't offer 978 tips, offer 1,000 or 1,001 tips).
- Incorporate keywords.
- Make it catchy.
- Match the tone and style of the title to the book.

Make it memorable, but for the right reasons.

UMB examples: What the . . .?

What do these books have in common?
- *The Theory of Lengthwise Rolling*
- *Oral Sadism and the Vegetarian Personality*
- *How to Shit in the Woods: An Environmentally Sound Approach to a Lost Art*
- *How to Avoid Huge Ships*
- *American Bottom Archaeology*

- *Greek Rural Postmen and Their Cancellation Numbers*
- *High Performance Stiffened Structures*
- *Butterworths Corporate Manslaughter Service*
- *Living with Crazy Buttocks*
- *Bombproof Your Horse*
- *People Who Don't Know They're Dead: How They Attach Themselves to Unsuspecting Bystanders and What to Do About It*
- *The Stray Shopping Carts of Eastern North America: A Guide to Field Identification*
- *The 2009–2014 World Outlook for 60-milligram Containers of Fromage Frais*
- *Crocheting Adventures with Hyperbolic Planes*
- *Managing a Dental Practice: The Genghis Khan Way*
- *Cooking with Poo*

The answer is, they're all winners of the annual *Bookseller*/Diagram Prize for Oddest Title of the Year.

This is one prize you really don't want to win.

The One-word Title

One-word novel titles are great – simple and powerful. But for non-fiction, you really need to convey more information than that. If I pick up a book simply called *Accounting* or *Cinema* or *Wellies*, I haven't a good enough idea of what that book is about. You either need to expand a one-word title, or add a subtitle (which online bookshops such as Amazon will simply run in the main title in any case); for example, *Wellies: The History of Welly-Wanging in Wales*.

The Gerund-to-start Title

A gerund is an *–ing* word – for example, *writing, believing, finding, thinking, doing, managing, perfecting, learning*. Starting a book title on a gerund is particularly effective for how-to guides, because you create a sense of ongoing action and immediacy, and convey that this book is really useful because the reader will *do* something with the contents. For example, I could have called this book *The Marketable Book*, but I didn't feel that clearly conveyed the point of the book; or *Write a Marketable Book*, but that sounds a bit bossy.

The Title That Brings in the Target Reader

If your book is for a specific audience, can you find a way to bring that audience into the title? For example:
- *A Parent's Guide to Potty Training*
- *Essay Writing for A Level Students*
- *The Mumpreneur's Manual for Workload Management*
- *Tips and Tricks for Keen Gardeners*
- *Stories for Seven-Year-Olds*
- *Basic Plumbing for Homeowners*
- *Persuasion Tactics for Salespeople*

The Does-what-it-says-on-the-tin Title

I'm a big fan of does-what-it-says-on-the-tin titles for non-fiction, especially how-to books, as you can see in three of my book titles: *How to Succeed as a Freelancer in Publishing*; *Survival Guide for New Parents: Pregnancy, Birth and the First Year*; *Writing a Marketable Book*.

Take *How to Succeed as a Freelancer in Publishing*. It's not a beautiful title. It's a bit wordy for my liking. But this is non-fiction we're talking, not literature – the title needs to be functional. The key elements of the book are that it's a *how-to* book, that it's about *succeeding* and that it's for *freelancers* who work in *publishing*. Because it's published by How To Books, the *How to* bit was essential. We could have stripped it down to *Freelancing in Publishing* – but then the reader wouldn't have a clue that this book is about really going places as a freelancer. We could have simplified to *Succeeding as a Freelancer*, but then that wouldn't accurately convey the scope of the material – freelancing within the publishing industry only.

Some other examples of clear, say-it-all titles:

- *Overcoming Depression For Dummies*
- *Jamie's 30-Minute Meals*
- *A Revolutionary Approach to Cooking Good Food Fast*
- *The Bike Book: Complete Bicycle Maintenance*
- *Gardening Secrets: From National Trust Experts*
- *How to Get Rich*
- *Property Matters: How Property Rights are Under Assault and Why You Should Care*

The Title and Subtitle Combo

It's very common in non-fiction to have a title and a subtitle, and I encourage you to consider doing so if you're struggling to fit all the key aspects of your book into one title. In title and subtitle combos the main title is the brief, in-a-nutshell hook, and the subtitle offers a little more explanation.

Here are some examples:
- *How to Walk in High Heels: The Girl's Guide to Everything*
- *Understanding Exposure: How to Shoot Great Photographs with Any Camera*
- *The Chimp Paradox: The Mind Management Programme to Help You Achieve Success, Confidence and Happiness*
- *In Stitches: The Highs and Lows of Life as an A&E Doctor*
- *Mindfulness: A Practical Guide to Finding Peace in a Frantic World*
- *Quiet: The Power of Introverts in a World That Can't Stop Talking*
- *Stephen Hawking: An Unfettered Mind*

Word to the Wise: Don't get carried away with a title and subtitle and end up with a stupidly long title. For example, Hilary Winston pushes it a bit far, in my opinion, with *My Boyfriend Wrote a Book About Me: And Other Stories I Shouldn't Share with Acquaintances, Coworkers, Taxi Drivers, Assistants, Job Interviewers, Bikini Waxers, and Ex/Current/Future Boyfriends But Have.*

Also avoid trying to improve your book's likelihood of appearing in a search on Amazon by stuffing the title full of keywords. Who wants to read *How to Lose Weight: Woman, Women, Diet, Diets, Skinny, Thin, Weight Loss Solution, Cellulite, Tone?*

UMB example: Selected Works of Nigel Tomm

The longest book title I've come across has 670 words. Amazon only fits in the following in its page for the book: *Selected Works of Nigel Tomm (2006/2007) (Shakespeare's Sonnets Remixed 2006 / Shakespeare's Hamlet Remixed 2007 / Shakespeare's Romeo and Juliet... Love Me Tender Remix 2007) Nigel Tomm is The.* Strangely, the book was out of print at the time of writing. To check out the full title, search for 'Selected-Shakespeares-Sonnets-Remixed-Hamlet' on Amazon.

The Biographical Book Title

Auto-/biography sits in the category of non-fiction, but in terms of title, you're best thinking along the lines of a novel's title (see Chapter 8). A good approach is to have a novel-type main title, and then a subtitle that spells out what the story is about. For example:

- *Call the Midwife: A True Story of the East End in the 1950s*
- *Gypsy Boy: My Life in the Secret World of the Romany Gypsies*
- *Out of Mormonism: A Woman's True Story*
- *We Never Lost Hope: A Holocaust Memoir and Love Story*
- *American Sniper: The Autobiography of the Most Lethal Sniper in U.S. Military History*
- *Once Upon a Secret: My Affair with President John F. Kennedy and Its Aftermath*

UMB examples: Terrible titles

- *Tables*
- *23.5 Reasons to Get Home Insurance*
- *This Diet Book Will Make You Lose Forty Pounds in a Week*
- *BBE Inputs into SYCY RBJs*
- *A Toddler's Guide to Getting a Mortgage*
- *The Greatest Love Story Ever Told: The Tale of One Man Who Lives Alone in the Peak District and How He Falls in Love with a Collie Dog and the Dog Finds Him When He Falls Down an Old Well One Day – It'll Make You Cry*
- *An Ensyclopeedeea of Ponie Saddles*

In a Nutshell

- Choose a unique title.
- Make it clear and concise.
- Convey exactly what the book is about.
- Incorporate keywords.
- Proofread the title carefully before publishing.

6. Content

What you write in a non-fiction book is your main concern. A reader may be forgiving of slight issues with style or structure; but no reader will forgive problems with your content – errors, omissions, offensive statements, improper use of quotations or plagiarism. Remember, a marketable book is one that pleases a reader. Use this chapter to check that what you're writing is what the reader wants to read.

Considering Your Reader

Chapter 4 helps you indentify the target reader for your book. Keep the reader in mind at all times when writing a non-fiction book.

The reader wants a book that's:
- Accessible
- Clear
- Engaging
- Factually correct
- Informative
- Interesting
- To the point
- Useful

The reader *doesn't* want a book that's:

- Contradictory
- Full of deviations
- Inaccurate
- Long-winded
- Over-complicated
- Patronising
- Repetitive
- Unbalanced
- Waffling
- Wordy

UMB example: Huh?

When choosing your offspring's educational establishment, and of course one must select a child's place of schooling otherwise the child will fail to have a school, one finds it uncumbersome and, indeed, most propitious to view said establishment in order that one might, forthwith, neglect to choose the offspring of one's educational establishment.

Knowing What to Include

Selection of material requires a balanced approach. You need to cover the subject thoroughly, without including details that aren't relevant.

Say you're writing a guide book called *How to Plan Your Wedding*. You need to cover all the main concerns for a bride-to-be and groom-to-be. So you include areas like the service, the outfits, the invitations, the venue, the catering and the entertainment. You wouldn't write a book on weddings without mentioning the cake, the wedding dress, the rings and the best man. But you draw the line at talking about how to meet a partner, how to convince a bride to make you maid of honour and how best to conceive a baby on the honeymoon – because this information isn't relevant. The reader doesn't want to know how to meet a partner; she's done that already, which is why she's planning a wedding. The reader doesn't want to know how to convince a bride to make her maid of honour, because she's the bride, not the bridesmaid. And the reader doesn't want to know how best to conceive a baby on the honeymoon, because that comes after the wedding – and this book is about wedding planning only.

Here's another example: you're writing a historical book about Kristallnacht, the series of shocking attacks against Jews carried out by Hitler's Stormtroopers on 9–10 November 1938. You include the key details of the event, and the antecendents and the consequences. You explore the reaction within Germany, and internationally. You examine how Kristallnacht affected the Jews. You consider Kristallnacht as a catalyst for the Final Solution. You situate Kristallnacht in the context of German and world history. But you restrain yourself from deviating from the focus of the book. So you don't include a 10,000-word biography of Hitler. Nor do you devote an entire chapter to the Reichstag fire of 1933, which allowed Hitler to consolidate his power.

Here are some points to keep in mind when selecting material:
- Research, research, research. Get to know your chosen subject intimately.

- Pick out the main aspects of a subject, and make sure you cover them adequately. When planning the book, spend some time with a pen and paper brainstorming all the main topics – then group them logically.

- Ensure that your content is balanced. If you're writing a book on Prince William and Catherine, Duchess of Cambridge, don't write twelve chapters on Will and only two paragraphs on Kate.

- Select the content that's relevant. Just because you know, in detail, exactly how a car engine works, doesn't mean you need to bore the reader with this info in your book *Setting Up a Car Valeting Business*.

- Keep focused on your reader. Write only what your target reader wants/needs. See the earlier section 'Considering Your Reader'.

Remember: Your mission is to create clear, useful content – not show off how much you know on a subject, or pad text to hide the fact that your knowledge in an area is patchy.

Conveying Your View

Think carefully about the viewpoint you convey in your non-fiction book.

Some books are very personalised, and clearly lay down the author's view on a subject. For example, you may write a guide to overcoming alcoholism based on your own proven approach. Or your book may be a memoir based on your personal experiences. In such cases, your view is the focus of the book (though it's still wise to be aware of other perspectives as well).

But for most non-fiction, the aim is to take a balanced approach that minimises bias. You want the book to apply to all your target readers, and explore a subject fairly and from all angles. Sometimes, that means putting your personal preferences and beliefs aside in order to be objective. For example:

- You write without judgement about disposable nappies, even though you only use reusables.
- You write without judgement about Tate Modern, even though you only like Tate Britain.
- You write without judgement about women in business, even though you're a closet anti-feminist.

Word to the Wise: If you want to create a marketable book, don't offend your readers. Write inclusively. Ensure that your book isn't racist or sexist or ageist or homophobic or any other –*ist*. For example:

- *Joanne Bloggs was only a housewife.* You've belittled Joanne, and annoyed every other housewife who reads the book.
- *Old people over 60 get a free bus pass.* Who wants to be called old? You've incensed an army of recently retired people who feel a long way from old age. In fact, you've probably annoyed most over-60s: that's about 10 million people in the UK.
- *An unnatural relationship, like that between two gay men...* Gay people (both men and women) are unimpressed. You've put off plenty of straight readers too.

Also take care not to stereotype. For example:

- *Teenagers are lazy.*
- *Pregnant women love pickles.*
- *Toddlers hate haircuts.*
- *Tories only care about themselves.*
- *Black people sing better.*
- *The French are argumentative.*

These may be your opinions, but they're not facts, so don't present them as such.

Quoting from Other Sources

Depending on the genre of your book, you may use quotations – extracts from other authors' works.

Use quotations sparingly. A book that's stuffed full of quotations says to the reader, 'This lazy author has cheated by borrowing loads of text from other writers.' Write in your own words where possible, and only use quotations where essential.

For example:

> *Summer 2011 'was a hot one' (James, 2012). According to the Met Office, there was 90 per cent 'less rainfall' between 'May and September' than 'fell in the same period in the previous' year (Met Office, 2011). '[T]here were lots of hosepipe bans' (Moore, 2012). As a result, plenty of 'lawns dried out' (Jones, 2011), and the* Daily Mail *reported that*

'3,000 frogs' living in 'wetland areas' died of 'dehydration'
(Daily Mail, 2011). In July, meteorologist Sam Murphy
stated: 'It's very hot weather, I'm sure you'll agree. I've been
fanning myself with a napkin. It's a frog-gone conclusion that
this hot weather will continue.'

Hard work to read, I'm sure you'll agree. Let's pick it apart:

- The quotes 'was a hot one' and '[t]here were lots of hosepipe bans' and 'lawns dried out' just aren't necessary – you can write these in your own words, without citing a source, as it's pretty basic information you can know for yourself.
- The quotation marks littered through the Met Office and 3,000 frogs sentences can be stripped out – just give the facts, and cite the sources.
- The quote in the final sentence has no attribution, and it needs to be stripped back so that only the essential part of the quote is used.

Here's an improved version:

Summer 2011 was hot. The period from May to September
saw 90 per cent less rainfall than in 2010 (Met Office, 2011).
Hosepipe bans were enforced and plenty of lawns dried out. In
addition, 3,000 frogs living in wetland areas died of dehydration
(Daily Mail, 2011). On 31 July, meteorologist Sam Murphy
stated on BBC News 24: 'It's a frog-gone conclusion that this
hot weather will continue.'

The *Oxford Style Manual* thoroughly explains how to use

quotations. Also check out the later section 'Using Quotations Fairly'.

Considering Legalities

When writing a non-fiction book, make sure you follow the law.

Avoiding Plagiarism

Don't pass off someone else's writing as your own. Plagiarising is bad form – and you're bound to get found out.

Certainly don't lift writing from sources and run it in your book without attribution as your own writing. I've caught several authors taking great chunks from Wikipedia and dumping these in their books. This is *totally* unacceptable.

If you really want to use a passage of text from source material in your book, the best approach is to set it as a quotation (see the earlier section 'Quoting from Other Sources'). Otherwise, you need to write in your own words. Ideally, you've done lots of research and can just write material based on the information in your mind – so the writing comes from you, no one else. But if you really, really can't avoid rewriting a passage of text from source material (paraphrasing), please take care that you rewrite adequately.

Remember: Rewriting means just that – writing it again, differently. You take the meaning of the source text and put it into new writing. Rewriting *doesn't* mean just changing the odd word: this is plagiarism.

Take this example:

> *Here's how you set up a new website: 1) buy the domain; 2) arrange hosting; 3) design the site; 4) put the site up online. If you want detailed information about visitors to your site, sign up for Google Analytics (www.google.com/analytics). All you need to do is add a bit of tracking code to the HTML of your website.*

Here's an unacceptable attempt at rewriting:

> *Here's how to set up a website:*
> *1) Buy your domain.*
> *2) Arrange some hosting.*
> *3) Design a site.*
> *4) Put the site online.*
> *If you want information about visitors to your site, get Google Analytics (www.google.com/analytics). What you do is add a tracking code to the HTML on your website.*

Here's an acceptable rewriting effort:

> *Setting up a website is an easy process. First you purchase a domain, and a hosting package; then you get to work designing the site. Once you're happy with the design, you launch the site online.*
>
> *You'll find it useful to know about the people who visit your site. Google's Analytics tool (available from www.google.com/analytics)*

allows you to add a simple line of HTML code to your website that keeps track of visitors.

Finally on the subject of plagiarism, take care not to mirror closely another person's book. Chapter 3 helps you ensure that your book idea is original.

USING QUOTATIONS FAIRLY

Under copyright law, you are entitled to quote material for the purposes of individual research, private study, criticism, review and reporting current events. You *must* acknowledge the source of all material you quote – as a minimum, the author's name and the publication or online source; but ideally also the year of publication and the publisher details.

Request the author's permission when you're quoting:
• An extract of more than 400 words
• A series of extracts that total more than 800 words, one of which comprises more than 300 words
• More than a quarter of the entire source material
• Any table, graph, figure or illustration – even if you're adapting it

For more information on copyright and permission, look at the *Oxford Style Manual* and also at the Society of Authors' *Guide to Copyright and Moral Rights* and *Guide to Permissions*, available online at www.societyofauthors.org/faqs-about-writing.

AVOIDING LIBEL

Take care that your writing isn't libellous. If you write a false statement (or one that you can't prove is true) that damages a person or an entity's reputation, you land yourself in hot water.

Be very, very sure of the facts before writing something negative about a real person/entity in a book. You must know that what you're writing is the truth, and be able to prove this.

Word to the Wise: Libel law doesn't apply to dead people. But don't take that to mean you can bash away freely at someone who's passed away. Tread carefully – you may be committing libel against someone connected to the deceased, such as a wife or business partner.

My advice would be not to write a book in which you're ripping into a real person/entity in the first place. It's a marketable book, perhaps; but not for the best reasons. And publishers are really reluctant, for obvious reasons, to take on books that may lead to legal wrangling, expensive law suits and reputational damage.

But if you really must write a potentially libellous book, your best bet is to consult a specialist libel lawyer before publication.

For more information on libel, request the *Libel, Privacy and Confidentiality* guide from the Society of Authors (go to www.societyofauthors.org/guides-and-articles).

The Special Case: Biographical Writing

Biography and autobiography read like fiction (narrative), but they're types of non-fiction writing because they're based on true events.

- A biography is a book written by an author about someone else's life. It usually starts at birth, and covers events through a person's life – either to the end point, death, or to the point at which the person is now. For example, *Coco Chanel: The Legend and the Life* by Justine Picardie.

- An autobiography is a book about the author's own life. It may start at birth, and cover events through the author's life – either to the end point, death, or to the point at which the author is now; or it may focus on a period in the author's life. For example, *Life and Laughing: My Story* by Michael McIntyre. Straightforward autobiography focuses on fact – a chronological telling of the story. Memoir, a type of autobiographical writing, is less about the bare bones of the story and more about the experience of events, especially the emotional impact then and now. As American author Gore Vidal explains in his memoir *Palimpsest*: 'A memoir is how one remembers one's own life, while an autobiography is history, requiring research, dates, facts double-checked.'

Although each falls under the category of non-fiction, because they take a narrative format, the guidance in Part 3 on writing fiction applies to these books. Biographical writing is a special case, because it bridges the two types of writing – so you need to understand both fiction and non-fiction conventions.

Here are some pointers for biographical writing:

- Do plenty of research and know the story and the person inside out.
- Identify the seminal events in the story, and hang the plot upon these.
- Move the book along carefully so it's an interesting, pacey read. You may decide the chronological approach of birth to end point is a bit staid. (See Chapters 7 and 11 for more on structuring.)
- Treat the subject of the book, and other people mentioned, as characters. (See Chapter 10 for more on characterisation.)
- Get a feel for the person's voice, and include convincing dialogue.
- Take care not to fictionalise – by all means make the book a good read, but not by inventing details that aren't true.
- Carefully consider libel issues (see the earlier section 'Avoiding Libel'). You may need to change names, places and so on. If in doubt, check with a lawyer.

Word to the Wise: If the book is about you, really think about the consequences of what you write. Your book may upset other people. And by opening yourself up and sharing personal experiences to the world, you make yourself vulnerable. Ask yourself as you write: Do I really want people to know this about me? How will people see me? How will publishing this book affect my life? How will publishing this book affect people I care about? If you have doubts about the book, don't dismiss them without thoroughly exploring them. You can't unpublish a book. Once your book is out there, you have to be able to handle the consequences.

MB example: *A Child Called 'It'* by Dave Pelzer

Pelzer's account of horrific child abuse became a worldwide sensation, and was at the number one spot on the *New York Times* bestselling list for six years. The success of his book spawned a massive wave of memoirs by abuse survivors. The marketability of Pelzer's book comes down to the extreme nature of the events (ideal fodder for the sensationalising media); the fact that Pelzer is inspirational in how he has moved past his terrible upbringing to help others; and his willingness to become a public figure.

In a Nutshell

- Write what your reader wants to read.
- Check your facts.
- Cover all aspects of a subject.
- Don't deviate into irrelevant discussions.
- Aim for balanced, non-judgemental writing.
- Avoid offensive statements.
- Don't overuse quotations.
- Know the rules for quotation usage.
- Don't copy other people's writing; write it yourself.

- Know what the law is on libel, and don't break it.
- Understand how biographical writing requires a balance of fiction and non-fiction approaches.

7. Structure

Chapter 6 helps you consider the content of your book; this chapter follows on and looks at how you organise that content with a clear, well-thought-out, logical structure.

Paying attention to structuring massively improves your book. Your structure is like a road map, guiding you in your writing and guiding the reader as she reads.

If you've read Chapter 4, you've already made a plan for your book. Now's the time to concrete your ideas and lay down a tight structure for the book.

Note: Biographical writing tends to follow the same structure as fiction writing, so skip to Chapter 12 if your non-fiction book is auto-/biography.

Taking the Time to Structure Carefully

It's clear to me from books I read that some authors pay little attention to structuring. They have a rough idea where the book's going, but they pretty much just sit at the computer and let the words flood out, hoping for the best. Why?

- Excuse #1: I don't need to think about structuring; I automatically structure as I write. You're one of the select few writers out there who can pay little attention to structuring and still turn out a superb book. You're a hugely talented writer whose subconscious mind auto-structures, allowing you to write a brilliantly organised non-fiction book without any thought. Are you really? Wow, that's awesome. If a tad unlikely.

- Excuse #2: It's not my job to structure; that's the editor's job. You bash a book out in a haphazard fashion, trusting that a freelance editor will tidy it up for you after the first draft is finished. Or – worse still – you bash a book out in a haphazard fashion, trusting that an agent/publisher will see past the structural issues and that a publisher's editor will tidy the book up for you. An unprofessional, lazy approach. You're the author; it's your job to structure the book expertly.

- Excuse #3: Structuring is too hard/boring/laborious. Yes, it is a bit of a slog. But some effort at the outset makes all the subsequent writing much easier. And you're less likely to need to revise the book over and over further down the road.

If you've stuck your head in the sand, ostrich-style, haul it out now. There is no excuse for shoddy structuring. Your structure should be clear enough that you know exactly where the book is going, line by line, and so does the reader.

Breaking Down Content

You can divide up your content in four ways:
- Parts: Groups of chapters.
- Chapters: Chunks of the overall book.

- Sections: Chunks of a chapter.
- Subsections: Chunks of a section.

Each part, chapter, section and subsection has a unifying theme. Take this book as an example:

- Part 5 is about what you do after you've written your book. All chapters in this part are on this theme.
- Chapter 18 in Part 5 is about what you do after submitting or publishing your book. All sections in Chapter 18 are on this theme.
- Section 1 in Chapter 18 is about assessing the success of your book. All subsections in Section 1 are on this theme.
- Subsection 1 in Chapter 18 is about assessing the success of your book if you approached agents/publishers.

Many authors simply use chapters to divide up the content in their books. It's entirely your choice, but books have clearer structures, and are therefore easier to write and easier to read, when content is broken down further. I encourage you to use sections and subsections within chapters of your book.

Remember: The split of the book into chapters and sections within chapters should help the reader gather, from a glance of the contents page, the key areas of the subject.

I like to follow the rule of having two or more sections or subsections – never just a lonely subsection. This leads to a better balance in the structuring. And I also avoid stacking headings, by which I mean having a section heading immediately followed by a subsection heading, with no text in between the two.

Working Out the Chapter Themes

You need to take all the information in your head, and in your research materials, and work out the key points of the book – the central topics. What are the core points you're making? What's at the very heart of the subject matter?

For example, say you're writing a healthy-eating cookbook. You brainstorm topics as follows:

- Information about healthy eating
- Benefits of healthy eating
- Spaghetti Bolognese recipe
- Cooking tips
- Pasta recipes
- Rice recipes
- Main meal recipes
- Meat recipes
- Fish recipes
- Vegetable recipes
- Dessert recipes

This is a starting point, but it's not a structure. Now, you carefully consider each aspect in turn, and you look at how you can build a structure from here.

So, you realise that the section on benefits of healthy eating is part of the section on information about healthy eating. And you think the cooking tips could slot in there too. You notice that Spaghetti Bolognese is a single recipe, not a section in its own right, so you move that to the pasta recipe section. You realise that while there are sections on mains and dessert, there's no section on starters, so you add that in. And then you rejig the sections into a logical order.

Here's an example of a structure you may come up with:
- Introduction, including information about healthy eating, the benefits of healthy eating and cooking tips
- Starter recipes
- Meat recipes
- Fish recipes
- Rice recipes
- Pasta recipes (including Spaghetti Bolognese)
- Vegetable recipes
- Dessert recipes

Alternatively, you may simplify the structure into four main sections – an introduction followed by sections on starters, mains and desserts, and each section has various subsections.
- Introduction, including information about healthy eating, the benefits of healthy eating and cooking tips
- Starter recipes
- Main meal recipes, broken into sections on rice, pasta (including Spaghetti Bolognese), meat, fish and vegetable recipes
- Dessert recipes

Toolkit: Get an A3 sheet of paper and some pens. Write the title of the book in the middle of the page and then start adding branches to key topics. Put this structure spidergram in your toolkit.

You're aiming for chapters that are a digestible length (not fifty pages) and chunky enough to really explore the topic (not three pages). You don't have to make each chapter the same length, but do try to balance the structure – so you don't have ten 1,500-word chapters and one 9,000-word one.

Also consider how you'll name your chapters. Many authors simply number a chapter; but you may also use a descriptive heading.

MB example: *Autobiography of a One-Year-Old* by Rohan Candappa

One of my favourite non-fiction books, marketable for its spot-on humour. Candappa has a lot of fun with structuring. The content (framed by an introduction and an outroduction) spans a year in a child's life, and is split down into months; then each month is split into chapters. Chapter headings grab the reader's attention (such as 'Sticks and Stones May Break My Bones But Honestly They Taste Better Than the Goo I Get Fed Most of the Time' and 'The Swing Thing: Towards an Understanding of the Addictive Qualities of Motion'), and Candappa uses short chapters intermixed with longer ones to good humourous effect. For example in the chapter entitled 'Sometimes I Do Things and Am So Wrapped Up in What I Am Doing That the Rest of the World and Everything in It Fades into Insignificance but Later On When I Look Back On What It Was That Engrossed Me I Have No Idea Why I Found It So Fascinating' the entire content is one sentence: 'I spent most of this morning running naked around a coffee table.'

Drilling Down into the Sections

Once you've worked out the chapter-by-chapter structure, organise the content of each chapter in turn. How you do so depends on the chronology of the subject matter (see the later section 'Considering Chronology'). For the cookery book, for example, you may arrange recipes in a chapter in alphabetical order, or cold ones first and then hot.

Toolkit: On the structure spidergram, take each chapter branch and split it out further into key topics. If you're using sections, these can form the sections of your book (and if you intend to use subsections, split the section branches out further). If you're flowing chapters as one body of text, it's still helpful to plan the direction of your writing in this way.

Try This: If writing the book in Microsoft Word, use heading styles to help you keep track of structuring. Style a chapter heading as Heading 1; a level 1 section as Heading 2; a level 2 subsection as Heading 3, and so on. Then you can either create a table of contents or use the Outline view, selecting heading levels only, to see the overall structure of the book at a glance. This is a great way to catch the odd heading that you may have mis-styled, accidentally creating a section, for example, where you need a subsection.

MB example: For Dummies guides

The hugely successful For Dummies brand is built on creating books that have great structures – clear, broken into bite-sized chunks, logically organised, no repetition, no fogginess or waffling. The author of a For Dummies guide works closely with the publisher's editors from the outset to organise the content of the book sensibly and carefully. Pick up any For Dummies guide and flick to the contents page. There you'll see, at a glance, the entire structure of the book laid down, from part to chapter to section to subsection.

Grouping Information

Try to group information on a particular topic, so that you cover one topic in one place only. For example, if you're writing a guide to UK taxation, don't talk about National Insurance contributions in five different chapters; try to include one thorough section on NICs in the book.

Grouping information sensibly stops you repeating yourself or spreading a topic so thinly that you fail to adequately explain it. When you cover a subject well in one place, you can simply refer the reader to that place in other parts of the book. For example, say you're writing a parenting guide. In Chapter 10, on bedtime routines, you write: *Bathtime is a good opportunity to check your child's hair for head lice. Chapter 5 on healthcare gives you the lowdown on how to spot, and eradicate, these pesky critters.*

When referring the reader to another part of the book, be specific. Don't say *Above, I mention xyz*, or *Later, I explain how to do xyz* – help the reader out and specify where you give this information. (Indeed, avoid *above* and *below* altogether for cross-referencing; often the text in question appears on another page, not above or below.)

Considering Chronology

When working on your book's structure, give some thought to chronology. You need a logical progression of ideas from one to the next – a subsection leads into a subsection, a section into a section, a chapter into a chapter.

Be especially careful with books that take a reader through a process. For example, this book is about the process of writing a marketable book. It begins with coming up with the idea, then explores writing the book, then publishing it, then marketing it – because this is the order in which you carry out the activity. It wouldn't make sense to start this book with a discussion of publishing options, then look at generating ideas, then look at book marketing and then look at writing the book – because book writing is a process with a start and an end, and the book is more useful to the reader if the content is arranged chronologically along that process.

Beginning, Middle, End

You're no doubt familiar with the idea that a story needs a beginning, a middle and an end. Well, non-fiction is no different to fiction in this aspect.

- Beginning: As a minimum, you usually include a contents page and an introduction that eases the reader into what the book's all about, how it's structured and who the author is. You may also have other material in the prelims (the publishing term for the first pages of a book), such as a dedication and a preface.

Acknowledgements can appear at the start of the book, or they may go at the end.

- Middle: This is the structure you've laid down by picking out the key topics and organising them into chapters.

- End: Sometimes a book simply ends on the final chapter, which rounds off the topic. Alternatively, you may include a concluding section – like an author's note. You may also include endmatter like appendixes, a glossary, references and useful resources for the reader. Many non-fiction books also have an index – you can do this yourself, or use a professional indexer.

Word to the Wise: Don't overload your book. A dedication followed by an epigraph (quote at the start) followed by a contents page followed by a list of illustrations followed by a list of tables followed by an author's note followed by a preface followed by an introduction… the reader's hard-pushed to get into this book.

Considering Length

How long should your non-fiction book be? Well, the answer depends on the nature and genre of your book.

You need to do your homework. Look closely at other books in the genre, especially competing titles (Chapter 3 helps you identify these). Count the words on five pages, divide by five and then multiply the result by the number of pages in the book to get a rough total word count. Also take a look at guidance on publishers' websites for the genre.

Bear in mind that what you need to achieve is a marketable length. Too short, and your reader feels let down and short-changed. Too long, and your reader is put off by the high cover price while a publisher is put off by the high printing costs.

Generally, an average book is around 50–80,000 words, but non-fiction can be considerably more (think textbooks) or shorter (think slim, quick-grab reference books). Around 55–65,000 words is a good target for a non-fiction book.

Toolkit: Once you've decided upon a suitable word length, make that your target. Split the total word target down by assigning a target word count for each chapter. Use the writing breakdown table you created for the toolkit in Chapter 4 to track progress against your targets. If your final book is a little over or under, that's fine – but at least you have a framework in place for ensuring the book will be a marketable length.

In a Nutshell

- Put thought and time into structuring.
- Break down content into manageable chunks.
- Divide content into key themes.
- Dedicate a chapter to each theme.
- Organise chapter contents logically and, where relevant, chronologically.
- Group information on a topic, to avoid repetition.
- Frame your chapters with a strong beginning and end.
- Research a suitable length for the book, and set targets.

Part 3

What You Write: Fiction

8. Coming Up with a Title

The title of your fiction book is either going to help or hinder its marketability. Get it right, and you convey to readers the essence of the book and pique their interest. Get it wrong and readers pass your book by.

With some books, the title walks into your head with the idea, and you stick with it. With other books, the right title is elusive or changes several times. This chapter helps you brainstorm ideas for a good, marketable title. I have split titles into types, but of course your title may tick several boxes – and if so, well done.

Remember: Once you come up with a great title, check that it's original. Type it into the Amazon search engine and see what comes up.

Toolkit: Add your final title to the toolkit.

Golden Rules for Titles

Before you get too carried away coming up with titles, remember that fiction titles must:
- Be catchy.
- Be original.
- Be pronounceable.

- Be interesting.
- Be relevant to the book.
- Contain no spelling, punctuation or grammatical errors.
- Fit on a book cover.
- Make sense.
- Not offend anyone.
- Suggest, but not give away, the story.
- Use language that readers easily understand.
- Make it memorable, but for the right reasons.

Word to the Wise: Unless you've a really clever use for it, avoid the word *adventure* in your book's title. It's pretty staid and cheesy.

The One-word Title

Summing up a book in one word is powerful. It's bold, it's clear, it's direct, it grabs the reader.

Here are some examples of one-word titles of bestselling books:
- *Alone*
- *Beloved*
- *Carrie*
- *Dracula*
- *Gone*
- *Hide*
- *Holes*
- *Intensity*

- *It*
- *Kindred*
- *Meridian*
- *Persuasion*
- *Room*

Remember: If you're going to use just one word for the title, make sure it really conveys what the book is about, and make it an intriguing word. Not something like *Also* or *Pharmaceutical* or *Hillock*.

The Character-based Title

Including your protagonist's name in your book title can work well. Examples include:

- *David Copperfield*
- *Deenie*
- *Emma*
- *Harry Potter and the…*
- *Jane Eyre*
- *Matilda*
- *Percy Jackson and the…*
- *Rebecca*
- *Robinson Crusoe*

If you're using your character's name in the title, it's even more important that you choose the name well. For example, if you've written a traditional romance novel and you want to have a *Romeo and Juliet* kind of title, it's not going to work if the lovers are called Fanny and Dick (well, unless you're writing a comic romance, or perhaps an erotic one). Flick to Chapter 10 for more on character names.

The Setting-based Title

If the setting is a major element of the book, you may decide to bring it into the title; for example:

- *Anne of Green Gables*
- *Brighton Rock*
- *Mansfield Park*
- *Private London*
- *The Tenant of Wildfell Hall*
- *Wuthering Heights*

The Somebody-somebody-and-the-something-something Title

I am, of course, talking about *Harry Potter and the Philosopher's Stone / Chamber of Secrets / Prisoner of Azkaban / Goblet of Fire / Order of the Phoenix / Half-Blood Prince / Deathly Hallows*.

This is an offshoot of the somebody-and-the-something (or something-something) title, like *Charlie and the Chocolate Factory* and *James and the Giant Peach*.

It's a nice format; it works well. But it's been done a lot – especially in children's writing. So take care not to copycat.

The XYZ Title

Titles that begin with *The* are popular, and they have a kind of gravitas and focus that's appealing. For example:

- *The Cat in the Hat*
- *The Da Vinci Code*
- *The Firm*
- *The Great Gatsby*
- *The Gruffalo*
- *The Hobbit*
- *The Kite Runner*
- *The Lord of the Flies*
- *The Lovely Bones*
- *The Way Forward Is with a Broken Heart*

Nothing wrong with a title that starts with *The*.

The Quirky Title

A great way to make an impact with the title is to choose one that makes a reader think, 'Eh?' For example:

- *A Clockwork Orange*
- *A Hat Full of Sky*
- *Divine Secrets of the Ya-Ya Sisterhood*
- *Nineteen Eighty-four*
- *Sea Otters Gambolling in the Wild, Wild Surf*
- *The Curious Incident of the Dog in the Night-Time*
- *The Elegance of the Hedgehog*
- *To Kill a Mockingbird*

Funny titles are also great – if a reader browsing in a bookshop spots your title and smiles, he's likely to pick up the book. Here are some examples:

- *The Earth, My Butt and Other Big Round Things*
- *Cloudy with a Chance of Meatballs*
- *So Long, and Thanks for All the Fish*
- *Garbage! Monster! Burp!*
- *Withering Tights*

MB example: Books by Christopher Brookmyre

One of the distinctive characteristics of a novel by Christopher Brookmyre is its attention-grabbing title:

- *Quite Ugly One Morning*
- *One Fine Day in the Middle of the Night*
- *Boiling a Frog*
- *A Big Boy Did It and Ran Away*
- *All Fun and Games Until Somebody Loses an Eye*
- *A Tale Etched in Blood and Hard Black Pencil*
- *The Attack of the Unsinkable Rubber Ducks*

Brilliant, aren't they?

The Inspired Title

Some of the best book titles are inspired by literature. For example:

- *Alone on a Wide, Wide Sea* (from 'The Rime of the Ancient Mariner', Samuel Taylor Coleridge)
- *By the Pricking of My Thumbs* and *The Sound and the*

Fury (both from Shakespeare's *Macbeth*)

- *For Whom the Bell Tolls* (from John Donne's 'Meditation XVII')
- *Of Mice and Men* (from the Robert Burns poem 'The Mouse')
- *Where Angels Fear to Tread* (from an Alexander Pope essay)

Also look to other art forms, such as art, music and drama.

The Title That Conveys Genre

You may choose a title that clearly conveys the genre of the book. For example:

- *Body Bags and Shallow Graves* says crime and murder.
- *Burning Embers* says passionate romance.
- *The Hitchhiker's Guide to the Galaxy* says science-fiction and humour.
- *The Unbearable Lightness of Being* says serious, philosophical novel.
- *Vampire Academy* says young adult and paranormal fiction.

The Excerpt-of-the-book Title

You choose a title from the text of the book itself. So, for example, Alice Walker's *The Color Purple* title is taken from a very powerful sentence whose meaning resonates through the book: 'I think it pisses God off when you walk by the color purple in a field and don't notice it.'

You can work the other way round and come up with a great title and then weave the words into the book.

The Book Series

If you're writing a series of books, you need titles that interlink. Here are some options:

- Have each title fit into an overall theme. For example, Stephenie Meyer focused on the moon/sun: *Twilight, New Moon, Eclipse, Breaking Dawn*.

- Use the same word across all titles. For example, Charlaine Harris's Sookie Stackhouse novels are entitled *Dead Until Dark, Living Dead in Dallas, Club Dead, Dead to the World, Dead as a Doornail, Definitely Dead, All Together Dead, From Dead to Worse, Dead and Gone, Dead in the Family* and *Dead Reckoning*. And Kathy Reichs has got a bone-thing going on in her book titles since the success of the TV series *Bones*: *Bare Bones, Cross Bones, Break No Bones, Bones to Ashes, Devil Bones, 206 Bones, Spider Bones, Flash and Bones*.

- Use a similar phrasing in all titles. For example, Stieg Larsson's *The Girl with the Dragon Tattoo, The Girl Who Played with Fire* and *The Girl Who Kicked the Hornet's Nest*.

- Create an overarching title for the series and simply have Book 1, Book 2 and so on. For example, Lemony Snicket's *A Series of Unfortunate Events*. This is rarely done – I'd recommend having a title for each book.

- Create an overarching title for the series and individual titles that tie together as well. For example, Cassandra

Clare's Mortal Instruments series, which comprises *City of Bones*, *City of Ashes*, *City of Glass* and *City of Fallen Angels*.

UMB examples: Terrible titles

- *Also*
- *A C**t of a Day*
- *Fiddleigglemunchamoonykin's Adventures in Dingleydooglyithmanepathland*
- *Intricate Botherism in a Cloudish Beautification of Objectification*
- *The Swell of the Ocean, the Pull of the Tides, the Salt of the Spray, the Sand Between My Toes: A Walk on a Beach on a Summer's Afternoon*
- *Jeremy Jingbot Falls Down the Crapper*
- *The Ghost of Smuggers' Inn, Which Turns Out to Be the Landlord Wearing a Sheet*
- *The Tiger, the Wizard and the Armoire*
- *The Dairy of Flicity Brown*

In a Nutshell

- Choose a unique title.
- Make it catchy and attention-grabbing.
- Keep it concise and to the point.
- Encapsulate the heart of your novel.
- Proofread the title carefully before publishing.

9. Setting

It was writer Rudyard Kipling who immortalised the basics of writing in his *Just So Stories* of 1902: 'I keep six honest serving-men/(They taught me all I knew); Their names are What and Why and When/And How and Where and Who.' Chapter 10 explores the *who* of fiction writing: characters; and Chapter 11 looks that the *what* and *why* and *how*: plot. This chapter focuses on the *where* and *when*: the setting for the book.

It's likely that when the idea for your book walked into your mind, with it came a sense of place. Indeed, it may even have been a setting that inspired the idea in the first place. This chapter helps you explore and develop the setting for your book, so that it goes from being a solitary place that exists only in your mind to one that a host of readers can visit too.

Understanding the Importance of Place

Often, when we read a book we pay little attention to the setting. It's there in the background, but we don't think much about it because we're focusing on the characters and the story. But place matters. The setting of your book is the basis for the story, the foundation that grounds the plot and the characters and helps to create the atmosphere.

Change the place in which the central action of your

favourite novel takes place, and you quickly realise how integral the setting is to the overall book. Imagine:

- *Bridget Jones's Diary* set in Mordor
- *Chocolat* set in Tokyo
- *Harry Potter* set in a Basildon comprehensive
- *The Life of Pi* set on the River Thames
- *The Great Gatsby* set in Antarctica
- *Wuthering Heights* set on a sunny beach in Dorset

The right setting makes a story real, tangible, vivid to the reader. When you choose your setting wisely, and describe it well, your reader is able to build a clear picture of the backdrop of the story – the scenery behind the actors in your play.

Seeing How Settings and Marketability Interconnect

Reading a book is all about escapism – journeying to another place in the mind. A marketable book, then, is one with a strong sense of place that successfully enables the reader to visit this other world in his imagination.

If you're approaching writing your book from a commercial angle, you may decide to choose a setting that's highly marketable, such as:

- A detailed fantasy world that enthrals a reader: Think Narnia and Oz and Discworld. JK Rowling's fantasy world is so popular an entire theme park has been created around it: The Wizarding World of Harry Potter.
- A real-life location that's well-known to readers: For

example, Paris, London, New York, Edinburgh. Even though readers may not have visited the place, they know plenty about it from other books and from film and TV.

- A real-life location that you think will help you market the book: For example, you may set a novel in your hometown, and look to push the book through local marketing. Or you may write a children's adventure set at a national tourist attraction, which agrees to sell the book in its gift shop.

Keep in mind your target audience – what setting will most engage the reader? (Chapter 4 helps you determine who's going to read your book.) And if you want your book to have international appeal, make sure you choose a setting that works for readers at home and abroad. So you may decide that a romance novel for teens is better placed in London, to appeal to US readers, than in Chipping Sodbury.

Creating Your Own Setting

Many authors choose to use real-life locations in their books, because doing so makes the story feel realistic to the reader.

But a common technique in books is to create a fictitious village/town (possibly based on a real one, or a blend of several real ones) within a real-life borough/county/country. The idea is that you create a generic backdrop that could be any town, thus allowing the reader to easily identify with and imagine the setting. (Think *Harry Potter*'s Little Whinging in Surrey, England.) This approach can be effective, especially in books with a fantastical or paranormal spin, but take care not to employ the technique simply out of laziness because you can't be bothered to research a location.

UMB examples: The fantastical setting in a novel that's grounded in realism

A chicklit book set in the fast-paced corporate world of Oxingaham; a political thriller set in the country Rabamorian; a historical novel about Mary, Queen of Scots set in Humdingerdom.

If your book is pure fantasy, you have the fun of creating a whole place for yourself in your mind. This isn't actually as easy as you might think. Make sure that you:

- Build up a solid picture in your mind. The reader needs to be able to sense, through your descriptions, that you really know the ins and outs of this world. Don't just make up the world as you go along – the reader can tell you're doing this. Take time before you write to imagine the place in your mind down to the smallest detail. Document everything you learn about the setting; this way, you won't slip into creating inconsistencies.

- Create a *realistic* fantasy world. This isn't always essential in children's books, but it is very important in adult novels. Readers want to believe in this new world, so make sure it's credible. Flying cars two years in the future? Characters chatting on mobile phones 300 years in the future? Women turning against men and killing them all? Sounds a bit unlikely to me.

An alternative to creating a brand new place for your fantasy novel is to alter a real place. For example, the city of Oxford appears in Philip Pulman's His Dark Materials trilogy, but the city is not as we know it today.

Deciding When to Set Your Book

You've three choices: past, present or future.

Ye Olde Booke

Books based in the past are popular. People are fascinated by history, and by the settings of yesteryear. A book set in Victorian London is often more romantic or thrilling or dark than one set in the modern-day city.

For books set in the past, do your homework thoroughly. Historical fiction must be rooted in fact. This guidance applies just as much to books set way back in time as it does to those set a few years ago.

Readers just love to spot mistakes and inconsistencies:
- 'People didn't say *simples* in 1810!'
- 'IVF in the 1930s?'
- 'Hang on, she's wearing a shellsuit. But it's 1973?'

- 'Tsk. The London bombings were on 7/7/05, not 8/7.'
- 'But if Tony Blair's still PM, it must be 2007, not 2008.'

Think carefully about society in the era. How empowered were women? Ethnic minorities? How was life different for rich people and poor people? What customs and expectations and prejudices existed in the society at this time?

You need to re-create a setting from the past in such a way that your reader doesn't question the details, but feels reassured that you know what you're talking about and enjoys having a realistic glimpse into this old world.

MB example: The Sally Lockhart quartet by Philip Pullman

The Ruby in the Smoke, The Shadow in the North, The Tiger in the Well and *The Tin Princess* are set in 19th-century London. Pullman expertly sets the scene – snuff, petticoats, opium, maids, sealing wax, hansom cabs. The settings are well researched and well described, and the reader finds it easy to picture the scenes.

WRITE NOW

Modern-day settings are the easiest to write, because you've the experience to do so and are less likely to slip up on the facts or get carried away in flights of fancy.

Factual accuracy still matters. If you're writing a book set in the year in which you're writing it, ensure that you include any relevant events. For example, if you're writing a diary-based novel set in 2012, your character can mention key events that occur during the year that are relevant to the plot, such as the London Olympics. Also make sure that dates and days are accurate, so if you write Tuesday 3rd April 2012, make sure that this date did in fact fall on a Tuesday.

If you know your book has a setting in the present, but the exact timing doesn't matter, don't pin down the timescale too tightly. For example, say you're writing a generic romance novel set in modern-day Guernsey and the exact year in which the book is set doesn't really matter. By all means give the reader an indication of the timing at the start of the book, but don't constantly refer to the date throughout the book. That way the reader is easily able to imagine the story in her present day, whenever that may be.

A Vision of the Future

Books set in a futuristic world are great fun to write, and science fiction is a popular genre. But the caveat I include in the earlier section 'Creating Your Own Setting' applies here: make the setting feel credible to the reader. The reader in the present day needs to feel that what you're projecting is actually possible.

Indeed, some of the best science-fiction writers have included futuristic ideas that went on to become fact. From Arthur C. Clarke's 1968 novel *2001: A Space Odyssey*:

When he tired of official reports and memoranda and

minutes, he would plug in his foolscap-size newspad into the ship's information circuit and scan the latest reports from Earth. One by one he would conjure up the world's major electronic papers… Switching to the display unit's short-term memory, he would hold the front page while he quickly searched the headlines and noted the items that interested him. Each had its own two-digit reference; when he punched that, the postage-stamp-size rectangle would expand until it neatly filled the screen and he could read it with comfort. When he had finished, he would flash back to the complete page and select a new subject for detailed examination.

Sounds rather like an iPad, doesn't it? Radar, escalators, submarines, tanks, virtual reality games, automatic doors, the atomic bomb, video chat – all these appeared in fictional books before they were taken to market.

Considering Types of Setting

There are as many settings as there are places in the world – and then some, when you factor in past, future and fantasy places. Here are some questions to bear in mind that can help you explore the setting in your mind:

- Advanced or undeveloped?
- Beautiful or ugly?
- Chic or shabby?
- Claustrophobic or open?

- Cold or warm?
- Colourful or drab?
- Familiar or new?
- Homely or uncomfortable?
- Light or dark?
- Modern or old-fashioned?
- Populated or lonely?
- Rural or urban?
- Safe or dangerous?
- High-tech or backward?
- Well-known or off the beaten track?
- Wild or tamed?

Try This: When thinking about where you're placing characters, step into the character's mind. See what the character sees and feel what the character feels. Is the character inspired, awed, comforted or liberated by a setting? Or frightened, frustrated, isolated, bored?

Thinking About the Places in Your Setting

In this chapter I talk about the setting of your book. By this I mean the central location(s) in which the story unfolds. The setting is likely to encompass various places. For example:

- In your gangster novel set in the East End of London, the action moves between various pubs and flats, a boxing club, a City bank and a greasy spoon.
- In your children's adventure book, half the action takes

place in a generic British village, and the rest takes place
in the fantasy world of Dingledell.

- In your horror novel, the protagonist hunts a terrible
monster across the major cities of Europe.

You need to carefully choose each of these places. Don't send
a gaggle of wealthy yummy mummies to have brunch in a
dodgy pub in Soho (unless the juxtaposition is deliberate to
make the characters uncomfortable). Place them in the cafe
on the top floor of Harvey Nichols, Knightsbridge.

Also think about how many places you incorporate in your
book. Setting connects closely to pace (see Chapter 11).

If you set your book, or a sizeable chunk of it, in one place
only – say a park or a village – you may struggle to keep the
reader's interest and keep the story moving along. Think of a
sitcom like *Friends*. If the entire episode took place in the cafe,
Central Perk, you'd get pretty bored just watching a load of
people sitting about talking. The producers of the show knew
this, so they moved the characters about to various locations
– their flats, their places of work, the park, the beach and so
on.

But imagine, on the other hand, that the producers had
used lots of locations, so the action in an episode flitted from
an apartment to a street to a park to a cafe to an apartment
to a street to a restaurant to a hair salon to a bar to a cafe to
a theatre to a museum to a cafe to an apartment to a taxi.
Phew; pretty exhausting! As a viewer, you'd feel quite
bewildered and struggle to connect to the settings because
there are too many, and they're too fleeting.

So, you need to work out the right balance between staying in one place and moving about in the book – depending on the plot and the genre in which you're writing.

Describing Settings

Some books have a stronger sense of place than others. Some settings require more description than others. Some genres involve more description than others. And some authors like to describe settings more than others.

How much you describe the setting is your choice. Too little description and your reader struggles to connect with the place and form a picture of it in her mind. Too much description slows the pace and interrupts the action, leaving the reader bored.

Take this setting description from the thriller *Alone* by Lisa Gardner:

> He was at the end of Newbury Street now, arriving at the Public Garden. Children were running through the maze of trees, trying to catch snowflakes on their tongues. Adults were out, too, bundled up against the cold. Some watched the kids. Others walked an assortment of exuberant dogs.

This is a thriller: fast-paced, suspense-full. So the author uses concise, tight description to set the scene. In a slower-paced, more descriptive book – such as literary fiction – you'd expect more detailed and poetic description.

Keep in mind that the way you describe a setting tells the reader about the narrator. Consider the first six sentences of Mark Haddon's *The Curious Incident of the Dog in the Night-Time*:

> It was 7 minutes after midnight. The dog was lying on the grass in the middle of the lawn in front of Mrs Shears' house. Its eyes were closed. It looked as if it was running on its side, the way dogs run when they think they are chasing a cat in a dream. But the dog was not running or asleep. There was a garden fork sticking out of the dog.

The simplicity of the writing and the selection of details to describe conveys a sense of the narrator, Christopher, who sees the world a little differently to most people due to Asperger's syndrome.

Try This: When describing settings, don't just focus on the visual aspects. Think also about noises, smells, sensations, even tastes. Appeal to the senses to help the reader easily visualise.

MB example: The Earth's Children series by Jean M. Auel

Jean M. Auel's Earth's Children six-book series is set in prehistoric Europe. The setting is absolutely fundamental to the story: the entire premise of the series is that these are historical fiction books exploring what life might have been like for our ancestors. So Auel describes the setting in detail (which explains why the books are very long; the last, *The Land of Painted Caves*, weighs in at 800 pages). The level of description isn't to everyone's taste, perhaps, but Auel's careful research blended with vivid imagination and her attention to detail have made her a bestselling and well-respected author.

Try This: Experiment with writing in different settings, to see how where you write informs the richness of the settings in your book. For example, you may find that spending some time writing in a cafe helps you write scenes in which characters are out in the hustle and bustle. Or to write a scene set amid beautiful scenery, you may sit in a park or take a drive out to the countryside.

In a Nutshell

- Put plenty of thought into the setting of your book.
- Consider how the setting can contribute to marketability.
- If inventing a setting, make it credible.
- Ensure factual accuracy in descriptions of the setting.
- Know how a character interprets the setting.
- Find a balance between staying still and moving about.
- Describe the setting well enough that a reader can imagine the scene in her mind.

10. Characters

Stories are about characters – be they people, animals, creatures or personified objects. A book without any characters is simply a description of a place – there's no story, no journey. Yawn.

People are interested in people. We read books to find out about people, to explore the people around us and also to explore ourselves as people. The better your characterisation, the more interesting your book, and the more interested the reader.

Understanding Types of Character

You can rank characters in books according to their importance and, consequently, what level of characterisation is required:

- Protagonist: Most books have a protagonist – the main character. The book may be told in the first person from the protagonist's perspective, or through third-person narration that focuses on the protagonist. The protagonist is the person around whom the story revolves. The protagonist is the most important character, and is the one you most need the reader to care about (see the later section 'Caring About the Central Character(s)'). You need to put a lot of effort into building this character; get it wrong and the book will flop. (Note: Some books don't have just one protagonist. For example, Josie Lloyd and Emlyn Rees's book *Come Together* alternates between the female and male point of view, and there are two main characters, Amy and Jack.)

- Central character: A central character is a step down from the protagonist, but is still important in the book. For example, take a romance novel told from the female point of view. The protagonist is the woman; her love interest is a central character. We need to know plenty about central characters, but we don't necessarily have to see the story from their perspective as we do with the protagonist.

- Mid-level character: These are people who are necessary for the story, but don't play a big part. Like the protagonist's parents in a teen novel. Or the investigating policeman who refuses to listen to the amateur sleuth hero of a whodunnit.

- Minor character: They have small parts, and so we don't need to know much about them.

- Extras: The bloke at the bus stop; the woman behind the counter in the fish and chip shop; the member of the crowd in the riot scene – the most we need is to see and hear them; we've no interest in who they are.

It's useful to have a clear picture of the character hierarchy, because this helps you devote the most space and focus in the book to the characters that are most important, and less to those that don't matter. So, for example, you slot in key elements of the protagonist's backstory; but you don't digress into the life story of a taxi driver who appears in one paragraph of the book.

Toolkit: On a piece of paper, draw several concentric circles. In the middle one, write the name of your protagonist. In the next one, write the names of the central characters. In the next, write the mid-level characters... and so on. Keep this hierarchy of characters to hand; it will help you check that you're giving the correct weight to characterising depending on the different levels.

Building a Picture of a Character

Really get to know your characters. It's not enough just to have a rough mental picture of a person you're writing about — know all about the character. Consider the following aspects and the examples of each that I provide:

- Attachment and attitudes to others — friends, family, lovers, acquaintances, strangers and so on
- Emotional place — happy, grieving, angry, frustrated, lonely
- Future plans — dreams, aspirations, goals, ambitions
- Intelligence — bright/average/slow
- Mannerisms — twitches, tics, habits
- Movement — graceful/clumsy, fast/slow, still/fidgety
- Noises — speech (language, accent, wordy/concise), voice (volume, tone), laughs, sniffs, coughs, sneezes, footfalls
- Opinions — political, cultural, social
- Passions — children, nature, culture, sex, learning, money

- Past – experiences, lessons learned
- Physical appearance – hair, eyes, face, skin, height, weight, build, stance, clothes, grooming, identifying marks (scars, blemishes, tattoos)
- Strengths – brave, positive, caring, focused
- Weaknesses – prejudiced, bitter, lazy, emotionally blocked

Give a character one or two identifying traits that remain constant through the book. For example, one character is fearless; another is brainy.

Toolkit: Start a character sketch file for each of the main characters, and add notes whenever you learn something new about the person. Use the character sketches to build up a detailed picture of the character that informs your writing.

Ultimately, you'll know a lot more about each character than the reader ever does. That's okay. Don't feel you have to cram every little detail that you know about a character into the book. In writing the epilogue to the final Harry Potter book, JK Rowling initially included lots of detail about the many characters. But then, she told *USA Today*, that 'it felt very much that I had crowbarred in every bit of information I could'. Her advice: 'In a novel you have to resist the urge to tell everything.'

Try This: Don't discard your character sketches; you may be able to use them further down the road. For example, post-publication you may share some of the untold aspects of a character on your blog/website.

Considering Character Names

Forget Shakespeare's 'What's in a name' logic; when it comes to characters, names matter.

Choosing names is a lot of fun. Depending on the plot and the genre, you may pick names that are:

- Comedic, to raise a smile; for example, Albus Percival Wolfric Brian Dumbledore.
- Common, to ensure the reader sees the character as a realistic, normal person; for example, Jane Smith.
- Foreign, to make a character more enigmatic or exotic; for example, Xavier de la Stade.
- Invented, to fit in the fantasy genre; for example, Denissa Wandermyst.
- Long and weighty, to convey the seriousness of a character; for example, Allessandra Charlotte Featherstonehaugh.
- Short and sharp, to pack a punch; for example, Tom Buck.
- Unusual, to be memorable and catch attention; for example, Marmaduke Tippex.

Word to the Wise: Don't use names that readers could confuse. For example, a reader may get a bit lost if the main characters are called Jim, Jon and Jo. Also beware of creating unpronounceable names such as Hiijauvenzjka. And check that you haven't inadvertently used a real person's name for a baddie – Dr Barry McTaggart won't be impressed if you've used his name for a dodgy GP character.

Caring About the Central Character(s)

Mike Twain wrote: 'The test of any good fiction is that you should care something for the characters; the good to succeed, the bad to fail. The trouble with most fiction is that you want them all to land in hell, together, as quickly as possible.'

The reader doesn't have to like a character necessarily, but the reader does need to care about what happens to that character.

If Hercule Poirot was a boring buffoon, we wouldn't bother to read on to find out how he cracks the case. If Bella in *Twilight* was an airhead cheerleader who was, like, grossed out by vampires, Meyer's saga would never have succeeded. If Harry Potter was a vicious hooligan, we'd quite happily accept Voldermort Avada-Kedavra-ing him.

Remember: Just because you care about your character, doesn't mean a reader will. Always consider a character from the reader's perspective. How does the character come across? I've seen authors get very attached to a character that, it emerges, is based either on them, or someone they know, and struggle to gain the perspective required to see that the character doesn't grab the reader.

Creating Realistic Characters

Your characters need to be believable. The reader must feel that this person could actually exist. That means that the character needs to walk and talk and move and think and feel and react within the realms of expectation.

Take a look at these examples:

- Jamie is from the mean streets of Los Angeles. He talks like this: 'What ho, chaps! Delightful evening, don't you think. Shall we dabble in a spot of car-jacking?'
- Joanne is a much-loved children's nurse who is cold and unpleasant to children.
- Barbara is a strict vegetarian on principle, but she cheerfully shoots a rabbit and hacks it up for her husband's supper.
- Bob is a detective inspector at the London Metropolitan Police who wears mascara and calls everyone darling.
- Angela is a devout Christian who uses the f*** word copiously in dialogue.
- Melissa doesn't give a fig about Doug throughout the book; in fact, he makes her skin crawl. But in the last chapter she saves his life and then kisses him passionately.
- Derek is a 57-year-old university professor who believes in the Easter bunny.
- Simon bashes his wife Mandy about. Mandy's not that bothered about it.

I could go on, but you get the idea. You set up a character, but then you undermine the characterisation. You create inconsistency and confusion.

Of course, people behave unexpectedly sometimes. Barbara the vegetarian may be having some kind of breakdown. Angela may have Tourette syndrome. If there's a logical explanation for a strange turnabout in your characterisation, and you show this clearly to the reader, that's fine. Just be careful that you aren't accidentally slipping into inconsistencies that push the reader's belief to the limit.

Characterising Villains

A villain may be an all-out baddie – a monster or a serial killer – or a less evil character who's standing in the way of the protagonist's happiness. Either way, villains are great to write. You get to bring out the deepest, darkest side of you and let rip.

Make your villainous character:
- Believable: The reader has to buy into the character and feel that this person could exist.
- More than one-dimensional: Pure evil is boring, and rather staid. More interesting are villains who aren't wholly bad; who have some weaknesses; who have a reason for their badness that makes the reader (unwillingly) empathise with them.
- Motive-driven: Few people are bad just for the sake of being bad. Naughtiness is motive-driven. Make it clear why the villain behaves as he does – is he out for money, revenge, glory, power, thrills, sexual gratification?
- Novel: Don't just go for Hollywood clichés; come up with a villain with a twist. Some of the best villains are the ones that aren't obvious; you think he's a nice chap until the last couple of chapters when – shock horror – he's revealed to be the evil mastermind.

- Powerful: The reader's not going to see the villain as much of a threat unless that villain has some measure of power.

MB example: *The Sculptress* by Minette Walters

Minette Walters' second novel, *The Sculptress*, was well received: 'A devastatingly effective second novel' (*Observer*); 'An exceptionally powerful and absorbing story' (*Mail on Sunday*); 'A stunningly good corkscrew of a crime novel' (*Daily Telegraph*)... The crux of the book's marketability is expert characterisation. Olive Martin, The Sculptress, is a deeply disturbing villain. Because, as reader, we're not quite sure what to make of her. We don't like her much. We don't trust her. But at various points in the book, we wonder whether we've got her wrong – is she actually an innocent victim? Walters effectively creates ambiguity around the character of Olive that is most unsettling for the reader.

Creating Flawed Heroes and Heroines

The 'goodies' in your book are the characters that you want the reader to like and champion. Danny's stuck in quicksand? Oh no! We hope Bingo the dog raises the alarm in time. Mr Gumpy's got five items left on his bucket list but he's feeling ropey? Hang on, mate! Melissa's torn between loving a fairy and a pixie? We hope she gets a happy ending.

But don't confuse creating likable characters with creating perfect ones. Just as you deepen the characterisation of a villain beyond inexplicable evil, you need to give your hero or heroine – lovely as he or she may be – some forgivable flaws. An impossibly good character is sickening, irritating, unbelievable. Make your characters human. So your protagonist may be shy or clumsy or geeky.

MB example: The Millennium Trilogy by Steig Larsson

Worldwide sensation. Bestselling books. Known worldwide. Award-winning. Hollywood blockbuster based on Book 1.

These are the kind of statements all authors would love to see attached to their book. So what makes Larsson's crime thrillers special?

Well, the central character, Lisbeth Salander, has a lot to do with it. She's gifted and troubled in equal measure, and she's as non-conformist as they come – pierced and tattooed; a computer hacker; socially awkward; bisexual; violent when challenged; sociopathic. The *New York Times* has called her 'a fiercely unconventional and darkly kooky antiheroine'. She's hugely flawed by society's standards. And yet the whole point of the book is that she isn't insane. She's as human as the rest of us.

Thinking of the Narrator as a Character

In a first-person narration, it's clear that the narrator is a character. The reader knows that when you write 'I walked across the room', it's the protagonist who walked across the room.

But third-person narration can be a bit trickier. For example: *Elaine walked across the room slowly, hips swaying sexily.*

God-damn but she looked fine. Who's writing this? The narrator. And the narrator is a character of sorts, because the narrator has a personality and a voice.

Think of how different narrators may say this line:

*   *Elaine walked across the room slowly, hips swaying sexily. God-damn but she looked fine.* Either the narrator finds Elaine sexy and beautiful, or the narrator is in Elaine's mind and is relating what she's saying to herself (this ambiguity isn't ideal, so in a novel you'd revise for clarity).
*   *Elaine walked across the room slowly, her hips swaying. Every man in the room watched her move admiringly.* Sounds like the narrator sees that Elaine is trying to look sexy and is succeeding in making men notice her.
*   *Elaine walked across the room slowly, hips swaying shamefully. She was dressed up to the nines, and sure enough, every poor sap in the room was drooling over her.* Sounds like the narrator is judgemental of Elaine's sexy walk and the men who appreciate it.

Toolkit: Note down a rough profile of your narrator – age, viewpoint, personality. That way you can ensure the voice remains consistent throughout the book.

Showing, Not Telling

Look to *show* the reader who a character is, rather than *telling* the reader.

So, for example, don't tell us that Anna is dull and has a tendency to digress; show us in some dialogue:

> *'So I said to him, and of course he listened… because he should listen… because men ought to listen to women… well, people ought to listen to people, I suppose, because it's a basic respect thing… did you know that Millie broke up with Max because he didn't listen?… so anyway I said to him, "Your tea's ready." And he said, "Thanks, love." Which was him listening. I think…'*

And don't tell us that Bert is grumpy, show him shouting at a child who strays into his path, or slamming his coffee mug down on his desk and scowling at his computer monitor.

Weaving in Character Information

In the first pages of a book, your job is to introduce the main characters and help the reader know who they are. This is a job that requires careful handling.

Take a look at the following methods of providing the reader with information about the characters.

METHOD #1: SHOVING IN PHYSICAL DESCRIPTION AMID ACTION

Take a look at the following opening paragraph from a novel:

The Nissan Micra stank. Taking a deep breath and holding it,
Mike eased open the glove compartment. Mike was 49, tall,
with broad shoulders and black hair going grey at the sides. He
had red cheeks from too much whiskey, and a paunch that caused
the buttons on his Thomas Pink shirt to strain alarmingly. His
eyes watered as he surveyed the sight before him. The withered
hand was bloated and seeping fluids.

Do you see the problem? The description is shoehorned into
a paragraph that's focusing on action – and interesting action
at that. By adding in the character's description here, the
author dilutes the drama of the stinky hand in the glove
compartment.

METHOD #2: HAVING THE CHARACTER LOOK IN A MIRROR

Here's another common way to dump in some description:

The Nissan Micra stank. Taking a deep breath and holding
it, Mike eased open the glove compartment. As he did so, the
reflection in the rear-view mirror caught his eye. The man
looking back at him was tall, with broad shoulders and black
hair going grey at the sides. He had red cheeks from too much
whiskey, and a paunch that caused the buttons on his
Thomas Pink shirt to strain alarmingly. Returning his gaze
to the glove compartment, Mike's eyes watered as he surveyed
the sight before him. The withered hand was bloated and
seeping fluids.

It's not a total no-no to have your character assess his own appearance, but it is rather clichéd.

Method #3: Randomly Digressing into Backstory

Back to Murderer Mike:

> *The Nissan Micra stank. Taking a deep breath and holding it, Mike eased open the glove compartment. It had been years since he'd driven a Nissan – back in the days when he and his brother would joyride for thrills on a Saturday afternoon. Growing up in the schemes of Glasgow as one of seven boys with an alcoholic single mother had been no picnic; no doubt that's why he'd never had a girlfriend, had spent two years in jail, was a diagnosed depressive and had once dissected a live sheep. His eyes watered as he surveyed the sight before him. The severed hand was bloated and seeping fluids.*

The author's condensed 90 per cent of Mike's character sketch into one sentence in the first para of the book, which really isn't ideal. As in the last two methods, the description is interrupting the action. And it's not relevant here – it's a tenuous link that the Nissan sparks a memory that creates narration of all this backstory. And, to boot, the author's given the game away: now we know that Mike is messed up and is no doubt responsible for the grisly contents of the glove compartment given that he likes to dissect live animals.

METHOD #4: BLENDING DESCRIPTION WITH STORY

Let's check in with Mike once more:

> *The Nissan Micra stank. Taking a deep breath, Mike leaned over his sizeable paunch and eased open the glove compartment. His bloodshot eyes watered as he surveyed the sight before him. The severed hand was bloated and seeping fluids.*

So we know two things about Mike from this paragraph: he's got a paunch and his eyes are bloodshot. And really, that's enough for this first paragraph. Other descriptions can be woven in later – for example, perhaps Mike gets some blood on his hand and wipes it off on his Thomas Pink shirt; perhaps he reflects on the gnarly end of the arm bone poking out and considers that he did a neater job on that sheep.

Certainly, you want some physical description – age, build, hair and eye colour – early on, to help the reader build a mental picture. But don't bury the early story development in an avalanche of character background.

Try This: Pick up a few novels, and read the first couple of chapters closely. Notice how the author tells you about characters. Which authors do it well? Which do it badly? Can you see what works best, and what's jarring or irritating for the reader?

> # MB example: *Dead Until Dark* by Charlaine Harris
>
> The Sookie Stackhouse series has brought a whole new level of sex, violence and intrigue to the vampire genre and led to the development of a widely popular TV show, *True Blood*. In the first book, after a few paragraphs of story, Harris blends in a physical description of her heroine: 'You can tell I don't get out much. And it's not because I'm not pretty. I am. I'm blond and blue-eyed, and my legs are strong and my bosom is substantial, and I have a waspy waistline.' To the point, enough detail for the reader to form a mental image, not so much we've lost the plot.

Taking the Character on a Journey

Novels are about characters going on a journey – physically, mentally and/or spiritually. Occasionally, a character is unchanged by that journey – for example, in a detective story the investigator may remain a constant character. But in most novels, the protagonist, at least, learns something through the course of the book – the story enables the character to grow and develop.

The journey may be from:

- Child to adult
- Emptiness to love
- Evil to goodness
- Fear to bravery
- Goodness to evil
- Ignorance to wisdom
- Imprisonment to freedom

- Isolation to company
- Naivety to experience
- Practical to creative
- Solitude to relationship
- Stagnancy to movement

Ask yourself: How do the characters in my book develop during the story? If the answer is 'not much' or 'not at all', think about whether characters are going to engage a reader effectively. If there's no journey in the book, the reader may struggle to connect to characters.

In a Nutshell

- Map out the hierarchy of characters in your book.
- Know all about a character.
- Think carefully about characters' names.
- Create characters that the reader cares about.
- Make sure characters are believable.
- Devise interesting, layered villains.
- Make heroes and heroines human.
- Show, don't tell.
- Weave in character information cleverly.
- Consider how your characters develop.

11. Plot and Structure

You've developed the idea for the book (see Chapter 3), and you've written a plan for the book (see Chapter 4), so you have some idea what the overall story is. Now you need to pin down the exact details of that story (plot) and decide how you're going to tell the story (structure). This chapter takes you through the *how* and the *what* of writing a fiction book, so that the story you write is engaging, interesting and, above all, marketable.

Considering Your Reader

Keep the reader in mind at all times when devising the plot of your fiction book. The reader wants a plot that's:

- Affective – exciting, scary, moving, cheering
- Clever
- Interesting
- Memorable
- Realistic
- Satisfying

The reader *doesn't* want a plot that's:

- Long-winded
- Over-complicated
- Repetitive

- Silly
- Slow
- Unbelievable

Remember: A marketable book is one that has a market and pleases that market. When working on your plot and structuring, try to see the book from the reader's perspective and consider what will make the reader turn pages rather than turn off.

Taking the Time to Structure Carefully

The guidance I provide in Chapter 7 on non-fiction structuring is essential for fiction writing too. Don't think you can get away with not considering structuring. Don't think it's an editor's job to structure for you. And don't skimp on structuring simply because it's laborious or boring.

Remember: Good books have well-thought-out, logical, clear structures that cleverly deliver the story and reassure the reader that the author knows where the book is going.

Breaking Down the Story

When it comes to structuring fiction books, you have various choices:

- Breaks: When you insert a break in a chapter – a space between paragraphs, sometimes with a symbol included, such as a row of asterisks (***) – you're signalling to the reader that there's been a shift in the plot. Usually, the shift is to a later time (so there's a gap in the action), to a sub-plot or to another character's point of view. Breaks are useful, because they allow you to move the plot forward and around. But take care not to overuse them, or the story jumps about.

- Chapters: Split a novel into chapters. Remember that each chapter needs to be a cohesive whole, with a good beginning and an end that either rounds the chapter off or leaves the action hanging, creating suspense. How long your chapters are depends on your writing style – try not to let them get overly drawn out or a reader can get bored. Use short chapters now and again if you want to create drama and suspense. And overall, try to have a rough balance to chapters; so, for example, you don't have one 8,000-word chapter amid a book full of 3,000-word chapters.

- Epilogue: The last section of the book that rounds off the story. The epilogue is set after the events of the story. It may explain what happens to characters, tie up loose threads and/or point to a sequel.

- Parts: You may choose to group chapters into parts. This works well if the story comes in stages, to denote major turning points and to separate the story where there's been a big shift in setting or time or characters (especially point of view).

- Prologue: An introductory section that sets the scene for the book. It gives background information for the coming plot, and offers a glimpse into the past or the future. It's a rather theatrical chapter, and some agents and publishers complain that it's overused. Personally, I like punchy, short prologues because they grab the reader's interest – which is essential at the start of the book.

Considering the Timeline

Writers like to play about with time because it makes a book more intriguing. Here are some options to consider for structuring your story if you want to try something other than simply telling it chronologically:

- Include a prologue with an extract from later in the book that hooks the reader by foreshadowing the action to come.
- Start halfway through the story and then skip back in time to build up to the start point before moving on to complete the tale.
- Start near the end, then flick back to the start and work through to the start point (take care not to give away the ending, though).
- Blend two or more timelines – for example, have one thread in the present and another in the past that's working its way chronologically through to intersect with the present plot.

MB example: *The Time Traveller's Wife* by Audrey Niffenegger

A best-selling book and winner of a Galaxy Book Award, *The Time Traveller's Wife* is an excellent example of multiple timelines. Read it slowly and closely, or you may get rather lost.

Word to the Wise: Whatever timeline you use, make sure you hold the book to it. For example, don't start the action on a Wednesday morning, run it through three days, declare you've reached the Monday and then later in the book say that the initial event happened in the afternoon. I see issues like this in manuscripts often. They're easily avoided by documenting the timeline in detail.

Toolkit: Set up a timeline log. Every time you move the action forward, note it in the log. Refer to the log as you write and you'll never lose track of timings.

Thinking About Point of View

Think about your favourite movie. Does the camera focus only on the lead character (let's call him Bill), seeing what he can see? More likely, the film includes all sorts of other footage too – a shot of the road outside Bill's house as he sleeps, a shot of a pan of water bubbling over unbeknownst to Bill as he chats on the phone, a shot of Bill's girlfriend in bed with his best mate while Bill's at work. All of these shots aren't from Bill's point of view; he can't know these things are happening.

In a movie, the camera is the narrator and has the power to go where it likes to tell us, the viewers, the story. In a book, the narrator is more likely to be the protagonist, or following the protagonist closely, which makes bringing in other characters' perspectives a little trickier.

Writing from multiple points of view in a book can make for an interesting, multi-layered read in which the reader gets to know what's going on inside different people's minds and in different locations. Say you're writing a teen fantasy novel. If you stay in the protagonist's point of view for the whole book, you limit the reader to knowing the facts only as the lead character discovers them. But if you weave in several chapters from the baddie sorcerer's point of view, you put the reader in a powerful position of knowing more than the protagonist about the overall story. This can make the book more interesting for the reader.

But as with time shifts in a book (see the preceding section), you need to handle movement between different points of view carefully. Take a look at the following examples and see whether you can spot the problem:

Tilly was tired. She hated walking to school. It was such a long way, and it made her feet hurt. I wish the car hadn't broken down, she thought. 'Come on!' said her brother crossly. What a weed, he thought. Tilly sniffed. She hated it when he snapped at her.

It's Monday morning and Clive is in a great mood. He sails into the office, beaming at his PA. What a beauty she is, he marvels. One of these days he'll have a slug of whiskey from the decanter on his desk, glide over and take her in his arms. Bethany, the PA, is worried by her usually-surly-boss's sunny demeanour and offers a wobbly smile. Clive is jubilant. She likes him! Hooray for this new Happifier drug.

I'm running but no matter how hard I pump my arms, pound my feet, gasp in breaths, it's not fast enough. He's gaining on me. I look behind. His eyes are maniacal, enraged. He's thinking about how she'll taste on toast; he's imagining her naked and helpless on a slice of Hovis. I run desperately, flying through the woods.

In each example, we're comfortably in one character's head, and then we're abruptly thrust into another character's before going back to the original character's perspective. Tilly can't know that her brother thinks she's a weed; Clive can't know that Bethany is worried by the change in him; the running character can't know that her pursuer is thinking about how she'll taste on toast. The point of view has shifted. Because these are short paragraphs, the shifts don't stand out too much; but imagine that a whole book is in the point of view of Tilly or Clive or the running character – the move into another character's mind is most confusing.

Even when a point of view switch isn't quite so fleeting, it can be jarring for the reader if you haven't established writing from that character's perspective. For example, you write a book in the third person focusing on the protagonist, Jenny, throughout. Her boyfriend, Dan, is introduced early on, and is always described from Jenny's point of view. But then, randomly, halfway through the book you include three paragraphs told from Dan's perspective, before returning to Jenny's.

As an author, you need to be controlled in how you handle points of view. Unless you're an experienced writer, you're best sticking to either one point of view in the book, or having a clear structure for moving perspectives – for example, you alternate points of view between chapters. If you want to try blending points of view and moving between them more often, you need to do so with extreme care so that the reader doesn't feel disorientated by shifts.

MB example: *The Collector* by John Fowles

This 1963 novel has become a classic in English literature. It's a simple, chilling story of a man, Frederick, who kidnaps a young woman, Miranda. The power of the book lies in the fact that Fowles allows us to get inside the minds of both characters, and explore the situation from the opposing sides. Fowles doesn't confuse the reader by flipping back and forth between points of view; he simply divides the book into three parts: Part 1 is told from Frederick's point of view; Part 2 retells the story of Part 1 from Miranda's point of view; Part 3 returns to Frederick's point of view. The use of multiple points of view is powerful, and I've no doubt the book would be much weakened without the author's expert use of this technique.

Weaving Together Plot Threads

Your book may have simply one perspective and one plot line running through. If so, that's fine – as long as the plot is sufficiently pacey and interesting to maintain the reader's interest.

But many books have more than one thread – a main plot, which follows the protagonist, and one or more sub-plots that follow other characters.

Multiple plot threads are great, because they add layers to the story and create a page-turning read. Say I've been gripped by a sword fight between two characters in Chapter 5. You leave the characters wrestling at the edge of a cliff and plunge me into a different plot thread in Chapter 6 – perhaps a princess escaping from the dungeon in which she's held. I enjoy reading Chapter 6, but in the back of my mind I'm wondering about the cliff-top battle. I know if I read on I'll find out what happens.

If you're really clever, you keep me on my toes throughout the book in this way – moving between threads, each time leaving me wanting to know more. What happens in the sword fight? What happens to the princess? Whatever thread you're writing in, I'm also thinking about the other threads and wondering where those parts of the story are going. See how involved I've become with the book?

Of course, not all books are full of suspense and drama as in this (cheesy) adventure novel example. But even a calmer book like a romance novel can benefit from multiple plot threads that create intrigue, suspense and layers of meaning.

Here's some guidance to bear in mind when weaving together plot threads:

- Do weave them together! Move between threads regularly so that the reader can keep track of the stories.
- Don't stuff too many threads into a book – I'd advise a maximum of three at any one point.
- Make sure the reader knows which is the main, overarching story, and which elements are sub-plots – focus more on the main tale, especially at the start of the book.
- Where applicable, cut off threads at a point that leaves

a question, so the reader wants to read on to find the answer.

- Don't drag out sub-plots – intersect them with the main story when it's time to do so, and then keep the action united in the main story.

Toolkit: Split a piece of paper into several columns. In the first column, write a flow chart of the action of the main plot; in the next column do the same for a sub-plot; and so on. Using a coloured pen, draw a line between events that intersect from one thread to another. Mapping the plots in this way helps you make sure that each is sufficiently developed (it makes sense on its own) and that they intersect. You can also use this chart to inform your chapter-by-chapter breakdown of the book.

Ironing Out Plot Inconsistencies

George has brown hair in Chapter 5, but in Chapter 10 it's grey. The door is left open when Mum and Dad head to the shops in Chapter 2, but when they return it's shut. The Wickham Wanderers win the match 4-3 in Chapter 5, but Chapter 12 says that the Wycombe Wonderers won that match 4-2. Readers are eagle-eyed, and they spot inconsistencies in your story.

The more complex your novel, the more likely it is that inconsistencies have crept in. Type 'Harry Potter inconsistency' into a search engine and you'll find plenty of fans arguing about JK Rowling's novels.

Your best approach to ensuring a clear, logical plot with no holes is to take a careful approach. When in doubt, look things up. Check that what you've written previously tallies with what you're writing now. Read the final book over and over. And ask others to read the book too – they'll spot things you've missed (see Chapter 15 for more on asking others for feedback).

Keeping Up the Pace

Some books trot along; some are a calm and gentle read. But whatever the fiction book, you need to pay attention to the pace.

Pace is the rhythm of your book. Think of your novel as a piece of classical music. Sometimes the music is loud and energetic and fast. Sometimes the music is slow and lilting and relaxing. A powerful symphony moves between loud and soft, fast and slow, building up and up before culminating in a cathartic climax. If you plotted the movement of the music on a graph, there would be peaks and troughs and an overall upward movement leading to a massive peak at the end.

Here are some pointers for pacing:

- Keep the book moving along. Long chapter after long chapter, paragraph after paragraph of description, lengthy episodes in which nothing much happens – all these slow a book, and you run the risk of the reader getting bored.
- Vary the pace. Stick a short, punchy chapter in after a

longer, slower one. Move between an exciting plot thread and a quieter one. Action after action after action can get dull – it's contrast between calm and drama that creates tension.

- Restrain the impulse to gallop. A canter does nicely instead. Genres like thriller and horror move along at pace, but don't speed through events without adequately exploring them.
- Head for The Big One. Your book may have a series of small climaxes, and that's fine. But make sure it's clear to the reader that you're building to The Big One. Don't run out of steam after your tenth mini-climax and end the book there. Readers expect a climactic ending.

Try This: Study films to improve your understanding of pace. A good starting point is a Hollywood blockbuster. Take the movie *Speed*, for example. It starts with high action – a lift about to fall. After the dramatic sequence, the movie slows down for a few minutes, and then goes into the next action – a bus exploding, a dash to get aboard a bus with a bomb on it. For the rest of the bus sequence the pace moves between a little tense to rather tense, before culminating in a majorly tense climax as the hero and heroine escape the bus. Instantly, the pace drops right down, before beginning the final ascent to the big climax – the hero versus the baddie atop an out-of-control subway train. The film ends a minute after the final climax. This is an action-led movie with plenty of tension that is sustained through keeping the story moving, varying the pace and using a series of small climaxes to build to The Big One.

Handling Transitions

A common issue that I see in authors' manuscripts is poor transitioning. The plot jumps suddenly, leaving the reader disorientated and confused. For example:

> *April was a beautiful month, balmy hot. Each day Alex and Francesca would dine outside on the patio, loving the feel of the sun on their skin after the long winter months.*
>
> *'You look beautiful today,' said Alex, looking fondly at Francesca over his prosciutto and plum tomato salad.*

Do you see how the plot jumps from generalised description about what Alex and Francesca did in April to a specific, undefined moment in time?

Here's another example of a poor transition:

> *The man was an idiot, Jane thought as she looked at her boss. How on earth had he got so high up in the company when he couldn't even sum a column in a spreadsheet? Every Friday it was the same: 'Jane, can you just…'*
>
> *'So, can you do this for Monday, Jane?' Mr Penderghast asked. She nodded reluctantly.*
>
> *'Jane? Is there a problem?'*
>
> *'No, sir. I'll sort that spreadsheet for you.'*

Sunday was a quiet day; she spent it combing her sheepskin rug.

One minute we're in the office with Jane, with a detailed, moment-by-moment account; the next it's Sunday and she's at home – a time shift has occurred, which throws us.

Think about the flow of your writing. Your narrator needs to lead the reader expertly through the story. Think of the narrator–reader relationship as being like that between Dickens' Scrooge and the Ghosts of Christmas Past, Present and Future. Just as the ghosts lead Scrooge through various scenes, where he's a spectator not a participant, so too does the narrator lead the reader through the story – logically and fluidly.

Considering Length

Decide on a target length for your book based on other books in the genre, especially competing titles (see Chapter 3). Count the words on five pages, divide by five and then multiply the result by the number of pages in the book to get a rough total word count.

Also take a look at the websites of publishers that publish books in the genre. Some stipulate, for example, that they won't take books longer than 100,000 words.

As a guide, young adult and adult fiction is usually around 70–90,000 words. Some books are shorter. Some are longer. For most books, I think between 75,000 and 90,000 words is a sensible length. Much less, and the story may not be sufficiently developed. Much more, and I wonder whether you're being heavy-handed enough in your editing.

With the growth of ebooks, it may well be that in coming years novel lengths change considerably. The length of a book to date has been influenced by print costs and the physical size of the book in the reader's hand (too thin and the reader doesn't think he'll get value for money; too thick and the price soars). Keep an eye on the market to see how book lengths develop; *The Bookseller* is an excellent source of information about the publishing industry.

In Chapter 7, I recommend having a clear word count target for the book, and breaking this down into individual chapter targets. But I don't recommend you use this strategy for writing fiction. Have a length bracket in mind, such as 80–90,000 words, but don't get too knotted up focusing on the word count.

Sometimes authors tell me happily, 'I've written 40,000 words now!' That's great, most commendable – but that doesn't mean those 40,000 words are final, ready to publish. At the polishing stage (see Chapter 15) you may cut out 15,000 words.

Remember: Focus on quality, not length. For your first draft, just write the story. Then you can assess how you're doing on length when you revise the manuscript.

In a Nutshell

- Write with your target reader in mind.
- Put time and effort into structuring.
- Break the story down into manageable chunks.

- Keep a grip on the timeline.
- Manage point of view shifts carefully.
- Balance and control plot threads.
- Avoid inconsistencies in the story.
- Ensure the pace of the book keeps the reader interested.
- Smooth transitions.
- Research a suitable length for the book, but for the first draft focus on quality, not word count.

Part 4

How You Write: Language

12. Writing with Style

If you read only one chapter in this book, I hope it's this one. Because no matter how great your idea, how carefully you've structured the book, how professionally you publish it or how cleverly you market it, if the writing itself – the mastery of language – isn't good, the book isn't good either.

American author Nathaniel Hawthorn hit the nail on the head when he said: 'Easy reading is damn hard writing.' Writing well takes a lot of creativity and thought and effort and skill. But when the words flow and you know – you *know* – they're good, that's the feeling that makes you keep writing; that's your very reason for writing.

Use this chapter to help you develop your confidence, your creativity and your technique as a writer.

Which Comes First, Substance or Style?

I've placed this chapter, and the subsequent two on aspects of language, *after* the chapters on writing your book for a reason. In my experience, the best approach to writing a book is to get the bare bones down, and then tidy and develop and beautify the language. If you attempt to make each sentence exactly as it should be as you write it, you lose momentum in the writing process.

Many writers find that, having planned the book, once

they create space for writing and get into the mood, the writing floods onto the page. This is exactly what you want. You're inspired! Don't waste time now trying to come up with a synonym for *treacherous*; in a few weeks or months, when you revise the book, you'll probably find it easy to think of a few words.

Remember: Editing yourself carefully as you write stymies the creative impulse, and you run the risk of losing your mojo and making the writing process slow and frustrating.

Developing Your Own Style

A writer's style grows from experience. The more you write, the more confidence you gain, and soon patterns emerge. Eventually, a distinctive, consistent style evolves.

Here's the same sentence, written six ways, to give you an idea of how styles can differ:

- *When going to a writing conference, take a pen and notepad with you to make notes.*
- *When going to a writing conference, take with you a pen and notepad so that you can make notes.*
- *When going to a writing conference, I recommend that you take a pen and notepad so that you are able to note down key points.*
- *It is good practice to bring a writing implement and a pad of paper to a conference on the craft of writing.*
- *Going to a writing conference? Don't forget your pen and pad.*
- *Writing conference essentials: pen and notepad.*

Passive or active. Formal or friendly. Prescriptive or suggestive. Concise or wordy. Questioning or informing. There are so many different styles! In the book you write, you need to use a consistent style; and it's likely to be the style you use in future books within the genre too.

For example, when I gave my husband the manuscript of this book to read, he told me, 'It's very you.' I asked him what he meant, and he explained that in all the non-fiction books I've written for myself (not ghosted), you get the same sense of me as author. It's a tone, a way of speaking through the book. That my writing style is established in this way makes him feel comfortable as a reader to pick up a new non-fiction book I've written, because he knows what to expect.

Now, while I've made certain style choices through my writing career, I never sat down at the start and laid down a concrete way of writing. My style has grown with me, and I've become increasingly confident in writing this way.

Developing your own style, then, is a matter of experimenting and experiencing. You need to explore how you most enjoy writing, what comes most easily to you, and go with it. The more your style develops, the more confident you become in your writing – and consequently, you write faster and better and with ease.

MB example: Meg Cabot

Meg Cabot is a great example of a writer with a clear style. She writes across genres – children's, romantic, paranormal – and for different age groups, from children to teen to adult. But pick up any Meg Cabot book and you'll see the same basis of writing style: the same wry humour, tight plot and lively characters. If I gave you five books without covers or any author information to read blind, and two were Meg Cabot titles while three were not, I bet you would easily match up the pair by the same author.

Meg's developed writing style is part of what makes her books marketable. If I read one book and like it, I'm very likely to read more – and there are over fifty to choose from.

Word to the Wise: One caveat on the subject of developing your own style is that when adopting an author voice that's not your own, you need to take care not to impose your own style on the book. For example, if the narrator of your book is a posh, formal, stuffy man, and you're a relaxed, happy, lively woman, you need to remember to put yourself in the man's shoes and write as if you were him. So you might write *It was a salubrious establishment, the very epitome of class, where no female dared bare so much as an ankle* rather than *It was a stuffy old place, full of hoity-toity blokes (though they were pretty fit), where the gals wore really long, ugly dresses.*

Writing outside of your natural style can be tricky. As a professional ghostwriter, I'm used to being a style chameleon. Here are the tricks I use to slot into a different writing style:

- Realise that the writing calls for a style that's different to your own.
- Carefully consider what comprises that different style. Think about the areas explored in the sections that follow.
- Adopt a persona as you write. If you're writing as a ten-year-old, try to act the character of a ten-year-old as you write – really get into the mindset of the child.

Considering Vocabulary

Use vocabulary that's appropriate to the subject, the tone and the target reader. So don't use words like *discombobulated* and *gentrification* in a simple how-to book, or words like *tits* and *arse* in a children's book.

Many authors get carried away with using flowery language in an attempt to show off their expertise in writing. Actually, the best writers are often those who write simply, not with affectation. In some kinds of writing, such as literary fiction and academic non-fiction, formal language that employs words not commonly used in everyday conversation may be preferred. But for most other forms of writing, you need to strike a balance between using the simplest form of English (called 'plain English') and seriously verbose, overdone writing.

Word to the Wise: If you're not sure what a word means, don't use it. If you don't know what it means, chances are the reader doesn't either. And who wants to wade through a dictionary just to follow the plot of a book?

UMB example: The swallowed-a-thesaurus approach

The matriarch debouched into the rathskeller, her altitudinous heels cudgelling an irascible, staccato beat on the igneous nadir. Her servant locomoted profoundly in her wake, promontory downcast, scapulas hunched grievously.

Occasionally, you need to use a word that the reader may not understand. For example, in a beginner's guide to tax you'd use words like *profit* and *loss* and *turnover*. You want to ensure that the reader understand these words – so make sure you define them the first time you use them. For example, *You need to work out the unique selling point (USP) of your book – the one, marketable aspect that sets your book apart from others.* In a non-fiction book, if you're using lots of jargon, consider adding a glossary.

Handling Repetition

Be aware of repeated words and phrases.

Sometimes, you use repetition deliberately, for effect. For example, *The dog was big. Really big.* That's fine – but don't push too far with such repetition: *The dog was big. Really big. He was so big he was elephantine big. Well, perhaps not quite. But still he was big. Big, big, big* Now the repetition is losing its impact and just irritating the reader. We get that the dog's big, now move on!

As well as repeating for effect, all writers repeat words and phrases without being aware of it – in sentences, in paragraphs and across the whole book. As a writer, you fall in love with certain phrases and words. So, for example, you may love the word *blatantly* or *ponderous* or *splendiferous*, or the phrase *conjures up a picture* or *at the end of the day* or *like a pig in mud*, and use it often. And because you're so close to the text, you easily miss the fact that you've missed the fact that you've repeated the phrase *miss the fact* thrice in a sentence.

The problem is that you don't notice the repetition, but the reader often does – and it's annoying. You want your reader to be lost in the content of your book, not distracted by the language. You want the reader to be thinking, 'Wow, this is exciting stuff. How is the grand master going to get out of this tight spot in time?', not, '*Suddenly* again. Jeez, that must be the fifteenth *suddenly* in this chapter. Why's everything so sudden? This writing's doing my head in. I think I'll bin this book and write a rubbish review of it on Amazon. Shame, looked interesting.'

So how can you minimise repetition?

- Read your writing back to yourself carefully, analysing each sentence and paragraph.
- Become aware of words and phrases that you use often. You're not looking for the basic words of the English language (like all the preceding words in this sentence) – you're looking for words that jump out to the reader, such as *meandering* and *humdinger* and *in a jiffy*. Keep a list, and do a global search for them in your book to check for repetition.
- Ask someone else to read your book and flag any repetition that he spots.

Avoiding Clichés

Try to write in your own style, without borrowing from other writers. Powerful writing is original.

Avoid stock clichés. There are many clichés in the English language, like the following:

- *As luck would have it*

- *At the end of the day*
- *Burn your bridges*
- *Like a knife through butter*
- *Pot calling the kettle black*
- *Pushes my button*
- *Rubbed up the wrong way*
- *You know what they say…*

Look to create your own, original, imagery. For example, instead of saying a character is running around like a headless chicken, you could say that he's running around like a toddler on speed; instead of saying someone's as sick as a dog, you could say that he's as sick as a vegetarian in an abattoir. Creating your own imagery really ups your appeal as an author because it shows you're a clever, imaginative writer, and it makes the writing more vivid. Plus, by inventing your own similes and metaphors you have a chance to tie them into the themes of the book and use them to create atmosphere. So, as an example, in a crime thriller you may weave in *cold as a cadaver* to describe the morning air just before the protagonist stumbles upon a corpse.

Structuring Sentences

It's beyond the scope of this book to get into the nitty-gritty of sentences – subjects, verbs, clauses and so on. But here's some guidance to bear in mind:

Short sentences are great for effect. For example: *He ran for the door. Damn! It was locked.* The short sentences create tension here, with a fast pace. But overuse of short sentences leads to stilted writing. For example: *I asked him why. He said nothing. I went to the window. I looked out. The sky was darkening. The sun bobbed on the horizon. Soon it would be night.*

The likes of Dickens could get away with very long sentences. Take the opening sentence of *Oliver Twist*:

> Among other public buildings in a certain town which for many reasons it will be prudent to refrain from mentioning, and to which I will assign no fictitious name, it boasts of one which is common to most towns, great or small, to wit, a workhouse; and in this workhouse was born, on a day and date which I need not take upon myself to repeat, inasmuch as it can be of no possible consequence to the reader, in this stage of the business at all events, the item of mortality whose name I prefixed to the head of this chapter.

We accept this rather rambling, digression-rich writing in 19th-century literature. But I wouldn't recommend this approach for modern-day writing for the simple reason that the reader can get lost.

A good approach is to mix up longer sentences and shorter ones. Reading aloud helps you get a feel for the rhythm of the writing – too many short sentences can create a staccato, jarring rhythm; too many long sentences can slow the pace right down.

Also vary how you structure sentences. Take a look at these examples:

- *Azhar crossed the road and entered the small shop. Azhar was looking for a diamond ring for his girlfriend. Azhar asked the man behind the counter for help.*

- *Unfortunately, the doctor had left for the day. Worriedly, Samuel wondered where he could get medical help at this hour. Hurriedly, he headed for the hospital.*

- *Grabbing her beach bag, she locked the car and headed down to the shore. Laying down her towel, she sat back and relaxed. Angling her face back, she basked in the warmth of the sun.*

Do you see how each sentence begins the same way? Pretty boring to read.

UMB example: *The Blah Story, Volume 4* by Nigel Tomm

There have been various contenders for the longest sentence in literature: James Joyce, *Ulysses*: 4,391 words; Jonathan Coe, *The Rotters' Club*: 13,955 words; Mathias Enard, *Zone*: 150,000 words. But the prize goes to self-published author Nigel Tomm for his one-sentence, 469,375-word book, *The Blah Story, Volume 4*. From the opening line: 'In a blah she was blah blah blah down a blah between blah roses blah blah blah, her blah blah hair blah blah gently the blah blah trees, most blah blah blah, she thought, as blah blah he blah the nice blah blah she blah felt'. And from the book description on Amazon.com: 'Overwhelmingly creative, Nigel Tomm demolishes the barrier of words and meaning, giving vitality and expressive strength to the pattern of his most exclusive novel – *The Blah Story*. It is a new way of conceiving text that frees the imagination, allowing you to personalize each and every word by your own creativity.'

In terms of marketability, Tomm did get noticed for this book –

it was featured in the *Guardian*, for example – but don't believe the adage 'all publicity is good publicity'. At the time of writing there was just one review for this book (published in 2007) on Amazon.com, which included the words 'I know the author thinks he's clever and arty and all that, but this is fifth grade stuff, frankly'. Hats off to Tomm for trying something new, but I'm not convinced this is a marketable book.

Structuring Paragraphs

A paragraph comprises one or more sentences that, together, form a self-contained unit on a particular theme or idea. If the paragraph contains more than one sentence, each sentence should logically follow the preceding sentence – so the idea flows through the paragraph.

Here's an example of a well-structured paragraph:

When he reached the end of the road, he looked back over his shoulder. The woods behind were dark and forbidding. There was no sign of the strange woman who had accosted him. She had disappeared into the thick shadows cast by the mighty oaks.

And here's an example of a poorly structured paragraph:

The room was quiet, eerily so. Jenny had long, dark hair and she wore blue jeans and a white shirt. The shutters were closed. The little daylight that filtered through the slats failed to reveal the contents of the shadowy shelves on the far wall. 'What are you doing?' The question startled Jenny.

In the first paragraph, each sentence flows from the next and there is one theme only: the woman in the woods behind. The second paragraph, conversely, jumps about. We start with a room description, then randomly skip to a physical description of a character, then back to a room description, and then – hello – there's a whole new character in the paragraph asking a question, and then we have Jenny's reaction. Phew! Pretty exhausting and disorientating to read, I'm sure you'll agree. Of course, this second paragraph is an extreme example, but I find issues with the flow of paragraphs in many books I edit, so it's certainly worth taking care in this area.

As well as looking at the logical progression of the idea within a paragraph, make sure that there are no jumps between paragraphs. Here's an example:

> *When placing your baby down for a nap, be sure to put his feet at the bottom of the cot. Doing so ensures he won't wriggle under the covers while sleeping.*

> *Dummies are great. I used dummies with all my children, and I'm sure they slept better as a result. We used to put several in the baby's cot.*

Do you see the jump between the first paragraph and the second? While reading the second paragraph, the reader is left thinking, 'So how do dummies relate to sleeping?' What you need is a smooth transition, or bridge, between the two paragraphs; for example:

> *When placing your baby down for a nap, be sure to put his feet*

at the bottom of the cot. Doing so ensures he won't wriggle under the covers while sleeping.

Also consider using a dummy to help your baby sleep well. Dummies are great. I used dummies with all my children, and I'm sure they slept better as a result. We used to put several in the baby's cot.

Notice in these examples that the paragraphs aren't too long. Long paragraphs are laborious and boring to read – whether the text is on an e-reader device or on a printed page, your mind finds it easier to digest small chunks rather than paragraphs that span up to a page or more. Break down long paragraphs into smaller ones. As a rule of thumb, I'd limit a paragraph to five sentences. But don't tie yourself up in knots counting; go by your eye – how the text looks on the page as you write it.

On the flip side, watch how you use short paragraphs, especially one-liners. Use them for impact, to catch the reader's attention. Don't rely on them too heavily, though, or you dilute the effect.

Remember: Apply a consistent format for paragraphs. Either insert a space between two paragraphs, or indent the start of each paragraph (but remember that text under a heading, or after a break, isn't indented).

Writing Clearly

A common problem in authors' writing is lack of clarity.

Sentences are vague and confusing. It's hugely frustrating for the reader.

When writing, keep asking yourself: I know what I mean, but does the reader?

Of course, context is key when it comes to clarity, but here are some examples of sentences that may require further development:

- *We put it down on the side.* Put what down? Who's we? What side – where?
- *It was given to me.* What was? Who gave it to you?
- *It all comes together in the chapter.* What does? What chapter?
- *All these things are the waves of life and loving that transition and up, with shimmers under the surface that ease us into realising the now; going to the past; as well as prepare for the days to come.* Huh? What do you mean?

Read your writing through carefully, and ensure that you're making your point clearly.

While thinking about clarity, also consider your use of the passive voice rather than the active voice. The passive voice is distant and vague; the active voice is clear and immediate. To help you understand the difference, here's an example:

- Passive: *The toys were given to the boys.*
- Active: *Mum gave the toys to the boys.*

Do you see that the passive voice is vague? You don't tell the reader who's doing the action. And this is frustrating for the reader, because it leaves a hole in the story.

Here are some more examples that show the difference when you change passive to active:

- *It was decided by him > He decided*
- *A mistake was made > Jim made a mistake*
- *A letter is being written by Uma > Uma is writing a letter*
- *It is said that the church is haunted > The villagers say that the church is haunted*
- *There is a considerable range of problems caused by criminals > Criminals cause a considerable range of problems*
- *We were invited > Sally invited us*
- *It's necessary to close the door > You need to close the door*

As you can see, the active phrasing is clearer and is often less wordy as well.

Writing Simply

Overwriting is a common problem for writers who aren't hugely experienced. If an agent quite likes your book but wants you to develop it further, overwriting is likely to be an issue you need to work on.

Basically, overwriting is over-the-top writing. You get so passionate about your book that you push the writing too far – it's overly theatrical, too flowery, repetitive. As the author, you're showing off. And the reader gets irritated.

Here's an example:

She stepped out onto the verdant, lush, oh-so-green grass, luxuriating in the sensation of the soft lawn beneath her bare feet, drinking in the emerald hue, breathing in the rich scent of freshly mown grass, enjoying the glint of the early morning sun on the beads of dew. Heaven! Pure heaven. Oh how she loved to walk on the luscious lawn after arising each morning, when the dew hung pendulously on the blades of grass – so wonderfully refreshing on her bare soles. Yes, indeed, she thought; I am a lucky lady to have so wonderfully wondrous a lawn.

The most powerful writing is often the simplest. You don't hide behind fancy words or strings of adjectives; you strip back your writing and let the naked core of what you're saying shine through. When you can control your writing talent in this way, that's when you write well and really engage the reader.

Making Every Word Matter

Every single word in your book should be there for a reason. If you want to write well then every word, every sentence, every paragraph should be carefully considered.

The worst writing I see is that which was been hammered out quickly and carelessly. As an author, you can become so focused on the overall body of work that you gallop along looking at the big picture, and you fail to drill down to the details of the book.

Pick up your favourite book – whether it's a children's picture book or an adult novel, a how-to-guide or a memoir – and look closely at each word. Do you see how much care has been taken in choosing each word and crafting each sentence? That's the marker of great writing.

MB example: *One Day* by David Nicholls

One Day is a hugely marketable book. It got rave reviews. It was made into a film. It was the bestselling book in the UK in 2011, selling 988,165 print copies, almost twice as many as the next bestselling book, Jamie Oliver's *Jamie's 30-Minute Meals* (source: *The Bookseller*). Why? Because it's a great, warm, true-to-life story. But, I would argue, most of all because of the quality of the writing. Forget speed-reading; this is a book that makes you slow down and really digest each word, because each has been so expertly chosen and placed.

In a Nutshell

- Get the bare bones down, then pretty up the language.
- Develop your own writing style.
- Tailor vocabulary for the genre, content and target reader.
- Avoid repetition.
- Go for fresh, original writing, not clichés.
- Keep control of your sentence structures, and vary them.
- Write neat, focused paragraphs.
- Ensure a logical progression from sentence to sentence and paragraph to paragraph.
- Write clearly, so the reader understands exactly what you mean.
- Pull back from overwriting.
- Make every word count.

13. Paying Attention to Spelling, Punctuation and Grammar

Mention spelling, punctuation and grammar (SPAG) to many people and they either break out in a cold sweat or yawn widely. I know it's not the most exciting or easy element of writing, but SPAG matters. A marketable book is a well-written, error-free book.

As an editor, I try not to be prescriptive. But when it comes to the English language there are some concrete rules you need to follow. An author once said to me he didn't bother with SPAG because it 'constrained his creativity'. Indeed. It also constrained his ability to get published.

In this chapter I give you some pointers to help you improve your spelling, punctuation and grammar, and avoid some of the common mistakes that authors make.

Try This: It's beyond the scope of this book to offer detailed guidance on SPAG. If you want to improve your SPAG, read plenty of language guides. I particularly recommend the Oxford series of guides; visit http://oxforddictionaries.com for details. You can also download the short ebook *101 Mistakes to Avoid in Your Writing* from my website at www.thebookspecialist.com.

Why Bother with SPAG?

If you're self-publishing, it's essential that your SPAG is correct. Readers will be distracted and irritated by mistakes. They won't enjoy your book. They won't recommend it to others. They'll write a negative review on Amazon. They may even make fun of you. There is simply no excuse for publishing a sub-standard book full of SPAG mistakes.

If you're submitting your book to agents/publishers, it's essential that your SPAG is correct. You want the agent/publisher to be impressed by your writing, your attention to detail, your commitment to quality and your professionalism. And you want to minimise work for the publisher, so it's that much easier for the publisher to say yes.

Of course, you can hire a professional editor to help you with SPAG. Indeed, I very much encourage you to do so, because unless you are a professional editor yourself, or a very experienced writer, you're likely to miss plenty of SPAG issues. But it doesn't hurt to improve your SPAG as well – because it means you're growing as a writer, and it means if you work with an editor on your book, her job is easier (which drops the cost of the edit). (For more on working with an editor, look at Chapter 15.)

Remember: The odd mistake is forgivable; a book riddled with errors is not.

MB example: Barbara Trapido

I recently heard Barbara Trapido – author of six books, three of which were shortlisted for the Whitbread – speak at an event. She explained that she'd made all manner of mistakes when writing and attempting to publish her first novel. But the one area in which she didn't make mistakes was SPAG. The publisher of her first novel changed only three commas in the entire manuscript before publishing it. Three commas. To put this in context, in a book I edit for a publisher I expect to make hundreds, even thousands of revisions. *Three commas*. The publisher must have been impressed by the quality of the writing.

Having a Positive Approach to SPAG

I'm a professional editor, so I've a finely tuned eye for SPAG mistakes. I notice them on signs, on menus, on Facebook statuses, on film credits. My sister bought me a lovely piece of artwork for my office that reads *Life is not measured by the breath we take, but the moment's that take our breath away*. I love it, but I do itch to add in the missing 's' and remove the unnecessary apostrophe.

My point is, there are SPAG mistakes everywhere. And you'll find no judgement or ridicule here for making mistakes. SPAG is hard stuff, and many people didn't have the best education in SPAG.

Two kinds of SPAG mistake exist:
- The mistake you miss. Everyone makes this kind of mistake, myself included. The only solution is to proofread and proofread and proofread some more (Chapter 15 covers proofreading).

- The mistake you don't realise is a mistake. That's where this chapter comes in. Not realising that a mistake is a mistake is no reflection of your intelligence or your writing ability. You just didn't know.

So don't worry about the current state of your SPAG. Just cast off memories of dreary English lessons and red-pen-wielding teachers, and enjoy learning more about the English language.

Remember: The best way to learn about SPAG is to learn by osmosis – read, read and read some more. Make sure it's quality writing, though, and not tabloid papers or trashy mags or blogs by people who think apostrophes are optional.

Improving Your Spelling

Spelling mistakes are the worst mistakes to make. A reader can overlook a missing full stop or a dodgy subject–verb agreement. A reader is less likely, however, to skip over a spelling mistake – especially if it's humorous.

UMB examples: Oops

In 2010, Penguin Australia was forced to pulp 7,000 copies of *The Pasta Bible* when it emerged that a recipe for tagliatelle with sardines and prosciutto included in the ingredients list 'salt and freshly ground black people'.

Also in 2010, American author Jonathan Franzen's novel *Freedom* was recalled and all 80,000 copies pulped when it was realised that the publisher had mistakenly sent to print the unproofread version of the book – which had around 50 SPAG mistakes in it.

In 2011 romance novelist Susan Andersen hit the headlines for an unfortunate spelling mistake in her book *Baby, I'm Yours*: 'He stiffened for a moment but then she felt his muscles loosen as he shitted on the ground.' It should, of course, have read *shifted*.

The media loved these stories, and no doubt that improved sales of the books concerned, which were reissued with the mistakes corrected. Still, I don't recommend taking as your lesson that spelling mistakes equal publicity that equals lots of books sold. You want to be known for being a great writer, not for embarrassing typos.

The following sections provide some guidance for improving your spelling.

Word to the Wise: Don't just rely on your spellchecker to correct all your spelling mistakes. It will miss many. By all means use the spellchecker, but carefully and with a degree of distrust.

Using a Dictionary – Often

Buy a big, chunky dictionary and refer to it whenever you're not sure of a spelling. Note down each spelling you look up. The act of writing it down helps cement the spelling in your mind, and you create a quick-reference guide for spellings.

Word to the Wise: Be careful with online dictionaries, which are often in US English.

KEEPING A LIST OF YOUR COMMON MISTAKES

Start to realise which mistakes you make often, and check for them. For example, you may automatically write *suprise* rather than *surprise*. Or you may often write *were* instead of *where*.

Try This: Do a global search in a document for common mistakes.

Toolkit: Add a list of your common mistakes.

BEING AWARE OF WORDS YOU COMMONLY CONFUSE

You use one word, but you mean another. The words are closely related, or they sound very similar. Here are the most common culprits:

- Advise/advice
- Affect/effect
- Bought/brought
- Breath/breathe
- Chose/choose
- Complement/compliment
- Enquire/inquire
- Except/accept
- Insure/ensure

- Lead/led
- Loose/lose
- Passed/past
- Practice/practice
- They're/their/there
- Warn/worn
- Where/wear/were/ware
- Who's/whose

KNOWING THE DIFFERENCE BETWEEN US AND UK ENGLISH

If you're writing a book for a UK market, write it in UK English. The following are some US English/*UK English* spelling differences:

- Analyze/*analyse*
- Center/*centre*
- Color/*colour*
- Defense (noun)/*defence*
- Fueled/*fuelled*
- Gotten/*got*
- Humor/*humour*
- Jewelry/*jewellery*
- License (noun)/*licence*
- Maneuver/*manoeuvre*
- OK/*okay*
- Skeptic/*sceptic*
- Skillful/*skilful*
- Theater/*theatre*
- Traveled/*travelled*

For a full list, check your dictionary.

Remember: Make sure your language on your computer is set to UK English – the spellchecker will then flag US spellings.

Punctuating Properly

The following sections take a basic look at the punctuation marks, and how to use them. For full details of how to punctuate, I'd recommend checking out the *Oxford Style Guide* and/or the *Oxford A–Z of Grammar and Punctuation*.

APOSTROPHES (')

An apostrophe indicates possession (as in *Charlie's book*), and denotes a missing letter or letters in a contraction (as in *I can't hear you*).

You don't need an apostrophe in plural numbers (1980s) or acronyms (PPEs).

Remember: The contractions *can't* and *don't* need apostrophes – *cant* and *wont* are words with different meanings.

Word to the Wise: Only use an apostrophe in *it's* when you're shortening *it is*. *The cat licked it's paw* isn't correct.

BRACKETS ( )

Ensure they come in pairs, and use curly ones (). Full stops come before the final bracket when the sentence is complete. *(Like this.)* Otherwise they follow the bracket *(like this)*.

COLONS (:) AND SEMI-COLONS (;)

A good number of rules govern usage. For full details, check out the *Oxford Style Guide* and/or the *Oxford A–Z of Grammar and Punctuation*.

In simple terms, a colon (:) is an introducer. It points forward and introduces:

*   A list (as above).
*   An extended quotation or direct speech. *Mr Jones says: 'I'm delighted by this promotion...'*
*   An explanation or amplification of the preceding part of the sentence. *There was only one thing to do: run.*

The last use is the one most people struggle with. Basically, a colon is a rather theatrical punctuation mark: it makes the reader pause and theatrically announces something to come that will add new information to the part of the sentence before the colon. Usually, the part of the sentence before the colon is a complete sentence in itself, and the colon could be replaced with words like *namely, that is, for example, for instance, because* and *therefore*.

The semi-colon (;) is a little like a comma but with special powers. It has two main jobs:

- It can join two separate sentences that are closely related. *It was his first job as a salesman; before this, he had been a teacher.*
- It can help divide up long and complicated lists that may otherwise be confusing. *I ordered a prawn cocktail, not with salad; steak, chips and peas; an ice cream sundae without nuts; and a pitcher of beer.*

Here's an example of choosing between a colon and a semi-colon:

- *The chancellor nodded; they had discussed this before.*

You want to connect these two sentences together, to show that the chancellor is nodding because he understands and he understands because they have discussed this before. You can't use a comma, because this would be a comma splice (see the comma section). You could possibly use a colon here, but it's not ideal – the punctuation after *nodded* is not meant to create a fanfare or signal to the reader 'ah-ha, now I'm really going to explain the phrase *The chancellor nodded*'. So you choose a semi-colon, which works perfectly.

Try This: If you don't feel confident using colons and semi-colons, simplify your writing so you use commas and full stops instead.

COMMAS

> # MB example: *Eats, Shoots and Leaves* by Lynn Truss
>
> Write a marketable book on punctuation? Well, that's exactly what Lynn Truss did back in 2003, and it became a *New York Times* bestseller, sparking a great public debate on English standards. The title exemplifies the importance of correct comma placement – a panda eats shoots and leaves; it doesn't eat, shoot and leave (eat and then shoot and then leave). The book is well worth a read if you want to use punctuation like a pro.

One of my favourite writing quotes is from Oscar Wilde: 'I was working on the proof of one of my poems all the morning, and took out a comma. In the afternoon I put it back again.' He hits the nail on the head, really. There are times when you know you need a comma, and times when you have to go by instinct. The best advice I can give is this: read your work aloud, and look to place a comma where you naturally pause.

Here are instances when you certainly need a comma:

- To denote that a word is missing. *Jenny had the lamb; Jamie, the beef.*
- When you have a list of adjectives. *She was a tall, thin, blond, ugly girl.*
- To offset a term of address or name. *'I'm not sure, Josie, that you like me at all.'... 'Darling, are you okay?'*

You may have heard of the Oxford comma, also known as the serial comma. This is a comma you can use before *and/or* at the end of a list. For example, *I gave him happiness, love, and encouragement; he gave me heartache, misery, and herpes.* The serial comma is optional. If you use it, use it consistently.

Word to the Wise: The comma is a weakling of a punctuation mark, and it's not strong enough to join two full sentences together. Consider the following sentence: *Jai took a breath, Mariette willed him to be silent.* This sentence actually consists of two separate sentences: *Jai took a breath* and *Mariette willed him to be silent.* You have three choices for how you avoid a comma splice, depending on the circumstances:

1. Split into two separate sentences: *Jai took a breath. Mariette willed him to be silent.*
2. Use a conjunction (*and, but* etc.) and join the two sentences together: *Jai took a breath and Mariette willed him to be silent.*
3. If the sentences are closely related, you can use a semi-colon: *Jai took a breath; Mariette willed him to be silent.* This works for this example, because the second sentence closely connects to the idea in the first – because Jai has taken a breath, Mariette is willing him to be silent. However, you can't join two sentences with a semi-colon if they aren't closely related; for example: *Ally is a great man; I like bananas.*

Ellipses (…)

An ellipsis indicates an omission in the text, and writers often use them to make a sentence trail off. Ellipses styling is up to you. You use three full points run together – closed up to the preceding text like this... with a space after; closed up entirely like...this; or spaced entirely like ... this.

Remember: An ellipsis never looks like this...............
That's amateurish writing.

EN DASHES (–)

Ensure that dashes are en dashes (–) and not hyphens (-). (They're called en dashes because they're the width of the letter N.) Microsoft Word will automatically create en dashes, but you can also use the keyboard shortcut ALT + 0150.

Use en dashes:

- In informal writing, to replace a comma, semi-colons or colons to emphasise, indicate interruption or signal an abrupt change: *I never liked him – but of course you knew that.* Don't overuse dashes used this way.
- For parenthesis (which means offsetting a phrase from the main sentence): *Ferdinand had an eye for such men – young, brilliant, handsome – and a talent for using them.*
- In ranges: *20–50.*
- To connect two words of equal weight: *North–South divide; Dover–Calais crossing; cost–benefit analysis; author–editor relationship.*

Exclamation Points and Question Marks (!?)

Don't use more than one exclamation point or question mark, and don't use both together. And try not to overuse exclamation marks – it weakens the effect.

Here's a common mistake: *Does every occurrence in your life have to have a reason, he pondered?* The question mark belongs with the question, not the entire sentence. Here's the correct version: *Does every occurrence in your life have to have a reason? he pondered.*

Hyphens (-)

Use a hyphen:

- To avoid ambiguity in what grammarians term compound modifiers – basically, two or more words before a noun that describe it; for example, *long-term aim, biggest-selling album, 33-year-old lady.*
- In two-word numbers like *twenty-one.*
- In terms starting with *self,* so *self-publishing.*
- To distinguish words spelled alike but differing in meaning, like *re-cover* and *recover.*

Don't hyphenate an adverb that ends in *–ly (happily, dreamily).* So *softly-voiced* is incorrect.

Quote Marks ("")

Use quote marks with dialogue, song titles and article titles.

You can use either double or single quote marks; just be consistent. Use single within double, and double within single; for example: '*And then he said "I hate you" in a horrible voice,*' said Sarah.

Avoiding Common Grammatical Mistakes

English grammar is a huge area. That's why it takes us many years, as a child, to learn to speak properly, and many more years to learn to write. I could write a whole book on correct grammar (but I won't, because that doesn't sound like a fun way to spend hours and hours to me, and against all the other books on grammar, I'm not sure it would be marketable). In this section, I stick to highlighting the most common grammatical mistakes I see time and time again in manuscripts.

- *A hotel* not *an hotel* (only use *an* when the word it precedes sounds like it begins with a vowel when spoken – e.g. *honour, hour, MP*).
- *A range of products is available*, not *a range of products are available* (the verb agrees with *range*, not *books – a range… is available*).
- *Because*, not *since* (in UK English).
- *Comprises*, not *is comprised of*.
- *Could have*, not *could of*.
- *Different from*, not *different than*.
- *He lies down on the bed*, not *he lays down on the bed*.
- *I'm not speaking to anybody*, not *I'm not speaking to nobody* (double negative).

- *Off*, not *off of*.
- *Sneaked*, not *snuck*.
- *Ten items or fewer*, not *ten items or less* (when you can count items, use fewer).
- *The man who*, not *the man that*.
- *The message was for both Chris and me*, not *The message was for both Chris and I* (remove the *both Chris and* part of the sentence if you're not sure – you can see that *The message was for I* sounds wrong).
- *Try to*, not *try and*.
- *Unique*, not *really unique* or *very unique* or *so unique* (something is either unique or it isn't).
- *Was sitting*, not *was sat*.
- *Was standing*, not *was stood*.
- *Would have*, not *would of*.

A note on pronouns. Strictly speaking, the following sentence isn't correct: *An author writes their book slowly*. The sentence should read either *An author writes her book slowly*, *An author writes his book slowly* or *An author writes his or her book slowly* (or be rewritten to read *Authors write their books slowly*). Some grammarians get hot and bothered about the use of *they* in place of *him/her*. But it's become increasingly common and accepted, and the oracle on the English language, Oxford University, permits the usage.

Try This: If you really want to brush up your grammar, grab a copy of *English Grammar For Dummies*. It's thorough and easy to understand (it had better be; I copy-edited it).

In a Nutshell

- A book submitted to an agent/publisher must have correct spelling, punctuation and grammar.
- A published book must have correct spelling, punctuation and grammar.
- SPAG mistakes in a book irritate a reader.
- Do your best to improve your SPAG.
- Be aware that you need a proofreader to ensure you've caught as many mistakes as possible.

14. Ensuring Consistency

Some elements of the English language are black and white. Rules exist that you must follow. For example, you can't spell potato *potattatoe*, just because you prefer it that way, and nor can you opt out of using full stops (see Chapter 13 on spelling, punctuation and grammar).

But other areas of language come under the umbrella of style, which is more open to personal interpretation. There are commonly agreed styles that you must adopt if you want to be taken seriously as a writer. And then there are styles for which you have an element of choice. What matters, above all, is that you apply a consistent style throughout your book. Being consistent shows you've paid attention to the language of your book, and you're writing at the level of a professional.

This chapter introduces you to some key elements of style, and helps you come up with a style sheet that you can use to ensure your writing is consistent.

Try This: If you really want to perfect your style, work your way through the *Oxford Style Manual*. It's a beast of a book, but it answers pretty much every question you come across on matters of style.

Toolkit: Create a style sheet on which you note down style decisions you make.

Abbreviations and Acronyms

Try to avoid abbreviations and acronyms in books as far as possible. *It was a long, lonely walk across the moors – a good four km, she reckoned…* doesn't read well for fiction. And non-fiction can too easily become cluttered with acronyms that are distracting on the eye and rely on the reader having read the one sentence in the book where you defined the term – *Take the RB and pop it in the SYD; now your DJI will BR with the CT.*

Here are some style tips:
- Don't use full stops if all the letters are upper case – *UK, BBC, NHS*
- You don't need full stops in contractions that take the first and last letters of a word – *Mr, Dr, Mrs, Ms, Revd*
- Use full stops in lower-case abbreviations like *a.m.*

Toolkit: Note down abbreviation styles you've decided to adopt on your style sheet.

Capitalisation

There are three types of capitalisation:
- ALL CAPS: Every letter is capped up.
- Sentence case (also called down style): Only the first word and proper nouns take an initial cap.
- Initial Caps: Most words take an initial cap (the explanation of exceptions is long and complex, so I'll stick to simply saying don't capitalise *a, an, the, and, but,*

or, for, nor or *to*).

Try This: Avoid all caps in your writing. Readers don't like to be SHOUTED AT.

Use initial caps for the following:

* A person's title when it's directly associated with the person's name: For example, *Prime Minister David Cameron made a statement today*, but *The prime minister made a statement today*.
* Mum/Dad when you're using the word in place of the person's name: For example, *I knew that Dad loved boats*, but *I knew that my dad loved boats*.
* Proper nouns: Names of specific places, people or things. For example, *Charlie*; *Edinburgh*; *the University of Nottingham*.
* Titles of works such as poems, songs, books and films: For example, 'That Still and Settled Place'; 'How to Save a Life'; *Writing a Marketable Book*; *Star Wars*.

Word to the Wise: Over-capitalisation is a common issue I see in manuscripts. Capital letters all over the place are distracting for the reader, they weaken emphasis and they indicate inexperienced writing. Unless you really need a capital letter, don't use it.

UMB example: The penchant for RANDOM Capitals

The King looked at his Courtier. The man must be LYING! How could the evil Duke have taken over the Palace? He had only been away since the Spring, dealing with those pesky Pixies. And the Queen had written him only last week saying that she was OK. Her Maid had delivered the letter. That fetching Maid; he'd like to ride THAT Horse. Hang on, come to think of it perhaps the glint he'd noticed in the Maid's eye when she handed over the letter hadn't been Lust. Perhaps it had been Evil intent. Good Grief! Was she in cahoots with the Duke? Was HE riding that Horse?

Toolkit: Note down capitalisation styles you've decided to adopt on your style sheet.

Dialogue

The commonly accepted style for dialogue is to place it in quote marks; for example: *'I don't know what you mean,' said Bob. 'Why would you think I don't love you? It's obvious.'* (Note: my italics here are to denote that this is an example; you don't need to italicise dialogue.)

Single or double quote marks? It's up to you. Single is the more common style in books published in the UK.

Toolkit: Note down the dialogue style you've decided to adopt on your style sheet.

Headings

Chapter headings and subheadings need to follow a consistent style. Chapter 1, Chapter 2; or Chapter I, Chapter II; or

CHAPTER ONE, CHAPTER TWO – it's up to you, just make sure they follow a pattern.

Try This: If you have a range of heading levels, use the heading style to show the section level – so move your way down in terms of emphasis. For example, you may have **CHAPTER HEADING**, **First Level Heading** and then *Second level heading*.

And while we're on the subject of headings, do check that they match up with the contents page, and that any numbering is sequential.

Toolkit: Note down the heading style you've decided to adopt on your style sheet.

Italicisation

The following should be in italics:

- Titles of works: Books, films, long musical compositions (such as symphonies and song albums), magazines, newspapers, paintings, sculptures, statues, plays, poems that can be published independently, ship names, television and radio continuing series (as opposed to single episodes, which go in quote marks).
- Foreign words: For example, *crème de la crème* and *que será será*. Check the dictionary; some go in Roman type because they've become mainstream English – like et cetera and déjà vu (note the accents – essential even in English). Don't italicise foreign place names and people's names.

You may also use italics for emphasis – although do so with restraint or you weaken the effect. And you may decide to use italics to differentiate word(s); for example, in non-fiction you may italicise a new term you're about to define, as in 'A *marketable* book is one that can be marketed'; or for examples, as I do throughout this book.

Remember: If you decide to italicise thoughts in a novel, only do so with direct thought – where you're writing from the character's point of view, not the narrator's. This is fine:

> She rang the doorbell and waited, shivering, on the step. *What if he's not home?* she worried. *If he's already left for the airport, I won't catch him in time. He'll leave without knowing I love him.*

This isn't correct:

> She rang the doorbell and waited, shivering, on the step. *If he wasn't home,* she thought, *it would be a disaster. If he had already left for the airport…* She realised then that *he may never know she loved him.*

Toolkit: Note down the italicisation style you've decided to adopt on your style sheet.

Numbers

Here are four rules for number styles:

- Don't start a sentence with a numeral – rephrase or write out. So say *Ninety per cent of mums suffer from exhaustion*; not *90 per cent of mums suffer from exhaustion*.
- Use a comma in numbers of four digits or more; so, *2,000*.
- Spell out the numbers one to ten.
- Don't mix numerals and words for the same or a similar group within a sentence: *Three girls and fourteen boys attended the class.*

In other areas you need to decide your own consistent style:

- Superscript: *20th* or *20ᵗʰ*? Personally, I avoid superscript because it feels a bit old-fashioned.
- Dates: Make sure they're in UK English – so number then month then year. You may prefer *21 December 2011* or *21st December 2011*.
- Times: I usually go with *9.30 a.m.* or *nine-thirty a.m.*, depending on the spelled-out/numeral rule.
- Spelled-out versus numerals: As a minimum, the numbers one to ten should be spelled out. Some authors may use numerals for 11 up; some may spell out all numbers. My preference in novels is to spell out all numbers, and to write 11 up in numerals for non-fiction.

Toolkit: Note down the number style you've decided to adopt on your style sheet.

Lists

In non-fiction books, you may have numbered and/or

bulleted lists. Whether you use numbered or bulleted lists is up to you. My preference is to use numbered lists for sequential and hierarchical material, and when the following text needs to refer back to one of the list items, and bullets for all other lists. Whichever you use, be consistent – don't use an a, b, c list on one page, then an i, ii, iii list on the next, and then a 1, 2, 3 list on the next.

Ensure that lists have a parallel structure. So each item in the list should lead logically from the introductory phrase before the list. The following list doesn't work:

Sandra had four aims:
- *To sell her house*
- *Moving to the seaside*
- *Learn to swim*
- *She wanted to be a writer*

This version has a parallel structure:

Sandra had four aims:
- *To sell her house*
- *To move to the seaside*
- *To learn to swim*
- *To be a writer*

Also ensure consistency of capitalisation. All full sentences in bullets start with a capital letter. You have a choice for incomplete phrases – lowercase or sentence case.

Be consistent with punctuation as well. Sentences end with a full stop. Phrases may end with no punctuation (as in the

Sandra example); a comma at the end of each item with a full stop on the final one; or a semi-colon at the end of each item with a full stop on the final one.

Toolkit: Note down the list style you've decided to adopt on your style sheet.

Spelling

In UK English, you can choose between the following spelling styles. It doesn't really matter which you use – just be consistent.

- *Among/amongst* and *while/whilst*
- *Anti-matter/antimatter* and *anti-freeze/antifreeze*
- *Co-operation/cooperation* and *co-ordinate/coordinate*
- *Dreamt/dreamed* and *learnt/learned*
- *Realize/realise* and *organize/organise*
- *Toward/towards* and *backward/backwards*

Toolkit: Create a spelling style quick-reference guide. Divide a piece of paper into a grid five across and six down. Put a letter in each square. Every time you make a choice on how to spell a word, note it down.

In a Nutshell

- Use a consistent style for abbreviations.
- Use a consistent style for capitalisation.

- Use a consistent style for dialogue.
- Use a consistent style for headings.
- Use a consistent style for italicisation.
- Use a consistent style for numbers.
- Use a consistent style for lists.
- Use a consistent style for spelling.

Part 5

After You Write: From Manuscript to 'Proper' Book

15. Polishing Your Manuscript

You type the last sentence of the book, sit back and grin. Hallelujah! Finishing your first draft is a great feeling – the relief, the sense of pride, the excitement of being able to see the book as a cohesive whole at last. Pour yourself a stiff whiskey or a generous glass of Rioja or a tumbler of guava juice, whatever your tipple, and toast yourself. By Jove, you've written a book!

Once you peel yourself off the ceiling, your next job is to realise that you've completed just one part of the journey to writing a marketable book. Publish your manuscript now and I guarantee you'll be disappointed by the outcome and embarrassed by the issues that you later spot in your book. Now, it's time to put away Creative You and welcome in Professional You.

It's time to polish your book until it shines.

Why Bother Polishing?

I very much hope you don't need to read this section – that it's obvious to you that there's a whole load of work to do after the first draft. But given the state of some of the manuscripts my colleagues and I see, it seems clear that some authors need guidance here.

No writer turns out a great, ready-to-publish first draft.

No writer. All writers have to spend a good deal of time and energy working on their manuscript to get it to the best possible standard.

Here's how the process works:
- You write the first draft.
- You edit and revise.
- You edit and revise.
- You edit and revise.
- You ask others for feedback.
- You edit and revise.
- You proofread.

At that point, say you send your book to an agent, who likes it. Here's what happens next:
- The agent makes suggestions, and in line with these you edit and revise. (This stage may repeat several times.)
- The agent secures a publisher, and the publisher makes suggestions, and in line with these you edit and revise. (This stage may repeat several times.)
- The publisher's development editor edits and revises.
- The publisher's copy editor edits and revises.
- The publisher's proofreader proofreads, and so do you. Again.

Phew! You see how much work it is being the published author of a marketable book?

Why do we bother putting so much effort into the book after it's at first-draft stage?

- Your first draft is likely to need plenty of work. There will be all sorts of areas for development, inconsistencies to iron out and mistakes to correct.
- You only get one chance to get it right with an agent/publisher. You can't send your book to an agent/publisher twice. You've got to impress them with your book. It must be as good as you can possibly get it.
- You only get one chance to get it right with a reader. If you self-publish a book, you're putting yourself out there as a published author. Publish a book that's not been sufficiently developed, edited and proofread and you damage your reputation. Yes, you can pull the book, rework it and then republish it, but by then it may be too late to hook readers.

Remember: A marketable book is a book polished to a high standard.

A Note on Professional Support

The preceding chapters in this book help you write a book. You do this all by yourself. But when you get to the point of polishing your book, it's worth bearing in mind that you can commission a professional editor to give you a helping hand with developing, copy-editing and proofreading the book. And you'd be wise to do so.

Publishers recommend that you do.
Agents recommend that you do.
Editorial consultants recommend that you do.

Remember: A marketable book is of high quality –
publisher-level quality. If you're not confident that you can
develop and edit and proofread a book to a professional
standard, you're best getting some support.

Years ago, in the days before the internet and the service
economy and self-publishing and ebooks, you may have
struggled to find a freelance editor offering services directly to
authors – they worked for publishers in the main. And there
weren't many freelancers, because a lot of publishers had in-
house editors.

In recent years, the publishing industry has changed
hugely. With more and more publishers outsourcing editorial
services to freelancers, the growth of self-publishing as a viable
route to market and an increase in the number of people
writing books (thanks, JK Rowling), there are now plenty of
freelancers available to hire.

This is good news, because it means you have access to
the professionals who work for publishers, and they have the
experience and skills to help you really polish your book.

But with so many editors offering their services, how do
you choose? Here's what you need to look for in your editor:

- Commercially aware: You want an editor who's got a
  keen eye on marketability.

- Experienced: You want an editor with a good
  understanding of publishing, who's worked with
  publishers and who's edited plenty of books.

- Good to work with: You don't want a dragon of an
  editor; you want to feel that the editor will be respectful,
  sensitive, supportive and friendly.

- Professional: You want to feel assured that you're

working with someone who's running a business of which you are the client.

Look for a freelance editor or an editorial agency that's professional and respected in the industry. Professional editors don't come cheap, but they can take your book to a whole new level and massively improve your book's marketability.

Getting Some Perspective

You've been writing this book for ages, and you're in the habit of dedicating time to the book. And you're very excited to have finished your first draft because now that tantalising finish line of publication seems close enough to touch. But before you blaze on and start fiddling with your manuscript, you need a break.

Stop.
Put your book away someplace safe.
Take some time off.

Go to the pub, go shopping, watch some trash TV, spend some time with your family. Do stuff that makes you happy *that doesn't involve writing or thinking about writing.*

Give yourself some breathing space from the book. Doing so allows you to shift from being the writer of the book who's immensely emotionally attached to each and every word, to the detached person who's savvy about the business of publishing and about what makes a good, marketable book.

Even just a week's space will make you a much better editor when it comes to your own writing.

Reading with Critical Eyes

Until now, you've been your own champion. You've had to have confidence in your writing just to manage sitting down and writing. You've believed in what you're writing. You've loved what you're writing. Your book has been your baby.

Now it's time to get tough, to look at your book from a fresh perspective.

Over the years I've worked with countless authors, and I've seen them struggle to look at their books with critical eyes. It's hugely difficult, I know. But if you want to polish your writing, to ensure your book really is marketable, you've got to be prepared to pick your book apart.

The bonus is, the more you work on polishing your writing, the more your writing improves. So, in time, your first draft gets better and better, and the revisions get less and less difficult.

Try This: If you really struggle to be critical about your writing, try to be critical of others'. Download or buy a book that you can tell by the cover and blurb isn't going to impress you (shoddy self-published ones are best). Now read it, and rip it apart. Really identify what's gone wrong with this book. Also take a look at Chapter 3, where I give you some questions to consider when reading books in your genre.

Editing Your Book

My editorial agency splits editing into two levels – development editing and copy-editing. Different publishers have different names for these editing services, but essentially these are the two forms of editing that a book goes through when it's published.

- Development editing is content editing, looking at all aspects of the book.
- Copy-editing is language editing.

Try This: Split the editing into these two levels. Do a first read where you focus on developing the book. Then do another read where you focus on language.

Part 4 gives you a good grounding in the language aspects of writing, and Parts 2 and 3 help you think about all the other elements of your book. Having worked through these, your book is hopefully in pretty good shape. But some stuff may have slipped through the net. So put the kettle on and make a brew in your 'Go Away, I'm Editing' mug (not got one? Shame – I find it an essential tool for editing…) and away you go.

DEVELOPING YOUR BOOK

Look through Parts 2, 3 and 4 again. Have you carried out all the guidance in these chapters? Look at these aspects:

Non-fiction:
* Title
* Content
* Structure
* Writing style

Fiction:
* Title
* Setting
* Characterisation
* Plot and structure
* Writing style

Work through each aspect of the book, considering whether there's any more work to be done.

As for other elements of book polishing, commission some professional support if you're struggling.

COPY-EDITING YOUR BOOK

Once you're happy that you've developed the book to its full potential, it's time to look at the language.

Read through the book carefully to check that language is:
* Accurate – prune out spelling, punctuation and grammar mistakes.
* Clear – the reader can easily follow your meaning.
* Consistent in tone and style.
* Fit for the genre and audience.

- Flowing – there's a logical progression from one idea to the next.
- Well-structured at the level of sentences and paragraphs.

Copy-editing your own book is hard, unless you're an experienced or professional writer. Once you've read the book through a couple of times, if you don't spot any more issues with language it's either because there aren't any (pretty unlikely) or you've reached the limit of your ability to edit (very likely).

You can read books on language, and there are some available on self-editing. But realistically, you're going to struggle to copy-edit at the level of a professional yourself. Your best bet if you really want to ensure a high standard of writing is to have a professional copy editor help you out.

Knowing When To Stop Editing

Editing plenty is good. Editing endlessly isn't. At some point you have to decide that the book is as good as you can get it right now, and let go.

Some authors become completely obsessed with revising their book. They tinker with it for weeks, months, years. They'll never know whether they've got a marketable book because they never get round to publishing it.

You may get locked into editing too much for two reasons:
- You're a perfectionist. You want your book to be perfect. Well, I commend you for having such high standards, but

sadly you'll never produce a perfect book. Say you write a book in your teens and publish it to critical acclaim, selling millions of copies worldwide. I guarantee that at age forty, with another ten books under your belt, you'll look at that first book and itch to revise it given all you've learnt about writing.

- You're procrastinating. Writing a book is fun. Publishing it is scary. What if it bombs? What if people criticise you? Much safer to sit at your desk and edit forevermore than take the next step and show the world your book.

There are two problems with over-editing:
- You'll never publish your book. And wasn't that the point of writing it in the first place?
- You'll destroy what's good in your book. When you get to the point that you're making changes just for the sake of making changes, you may well be stripping out great writing and replacing it with not-so-great writing. Stop! Put that red pen down!

Listen to your instincts. You know when you're happy with writing and are just editing for the sake of it, and when there's genuinely more work to do.

Try This: Don't discard previous versions of your book. Each time you re-edit, save it as a new document. That way, if you cut out Mr Muffin's daring tap dance atop a caravan in Edit 1, you can easily reinstate it in Edit 2 if you want.

Asking Others for Feedback

Once you're at a point where you don't feel you can do any more to your book, I recommend that you ask other people to take a look.

Scary stuff! What if they hate it? What if they just don't get it? What if they say stuff that hurts you?

It is hard, I know. As experienced as I am, there are always butterflies in my tummy when I finally let someone read my new book. But if you want to be a published author, you're going to have to get brave and grow a thick skin.

Remember: Feedback is essential – but it only works if you actually take on board the feedback! Don't ask people to read your book if you're not prepared to listen to their comments. You might not like what they say, but note it down: it's valuable for developing your book.

DECIDING WHICH PEOPLE TO ASK

So, who can give you useful feedback? It's pretty much the same list I give you in Chapter 2 when considering people you can approach about your book idea. But here, if your budget can stretch, I highly recommend getting a professional opinion.

Your mum, your best friend, your wife, your secretary – they'll all be dead impressed that you've written a book and, because they care about you, they'll tell you it's brilliant. That's lovely, confidence-building, comforting feedback – but it's not necessarily truthful or accurate.

What you need is someone who knows all about books, and who doesn't have any emotional investment in telling what you want to hear, to look at your book and give you some diplomatic but honest feedback. A *book critique* sounds horribly critical, I know; however, the aim isn't to criticise, but to help you develop your book.

I've assessed hundreds of books over the years. Occasionally, I've told an author that I believe her book is amazing, fabulous, wonderful, and that she should send it straight out to publishers. Sometimes, I've told an author that I don't think her book has any chance of being published or, if self-published, selling well. And sometimes – often – I've suggested development to the book which will improve it and make it more marketable.

The fear that holds many authors back from getting a professional opinion is that they'll be told they should give up on the book – that it's just no good. If you've effectively and carefully followed the guidance in this book, that's not going to happen. But if something's gone awry and you have produced a total doozy of a book, isn't it better to know that at this stage, rather than spend the next year submitting it to agents/publishers or self-publishing it and marketing it to no avail?

Remember: When it comes to publishing, you only get one shot. Send out a flawed manuscript to agents/publishers and you may miss your chance. Publish a book that's not at its best and you'll get poor sales and damage your credibility as an author.

Moving Forward After Feedback

If you seek feedback on your book (and I hope you do), you reach a point where you have to decide what to do with it.

- If you've commissioned a professional to give you feedback, you need to develop your book in line with the editor's recommendations. If you really, really, really disagree with a recommendation, talk to the editor about that. But overall, you need to trust your editor. She knows what she's doing: it's her job!

- If you're wondering what to do with feedback from other people, your best bet is to use common sense and to follow your gut instincts. If four out of the five people who've read your book told you they found it hard to get into, you need to revise the beginning. If one reader told you he was struggling to follow some of the concepts you explain, even though four people seemed to manage okay, you may revise the book to ensure it's always clear and accessible. But if a reader told you he didn't like the setting (London) and thought in fact you should set the book in his hometown (Slough), you hopefully realise that's just his opinion and that he's completely missed the point that a novel focusing on politicians in Parliament needs to take place in London.

Try This: When you first get feedback on your book, do nothing with it. Give yourself a few days to sit with the feedback. Especially if the feedback had some negative aspects, you may have an initial, emotional reaction that clouds your judgement. *How dare he tell me my protagonist isn't* *likeable? I adore him!* In a few days, with some perspective, you may look again at your lead character and see how a reader could misunderstand him. Excellent; you've a good basis now to work on that character.

Proofreading

Proofreading weeds out spelling, grammar and punctuation mistakes, and inconsistencies in your book.

Proofreading is absolutely essential. There's simply no excuse for publishing a book full of typos and poor grammar and punctuation that an eight-year-old would scoff at.

If you want to be taken seriously as an author, you need to take proofreading seriously. Strange as it seems, a reader is more likely to forgive a character that's poorly developed or content that's chaotic than they are to forgive lots of spelling mistakes. Nothing shouts 'amateur author' as loud as SPAG issues (spelling, punctuation and grammar).

Some of the authors who've recently sold aplenty on Amazon via self-publishing have a complete disregard for proofreading. Not good enough in my book (excuse the pun). Quality matters. You want to create a marketable book, and this may well be the first of many marketable books. To achieve your dream, your readers must think your books are the bees' knees. Not: *Well, the book is pretty good. Shame about all the typos.*

Sermon over. Now, how can you successfully proofread your book? Confession: that was a trick question. You, alone, are going to struggle to proofread your book. There's plenty you can do – and I'll give you some top tips shortly – but realistically, you need a second (and perhaps a third) pair of eyes.

Getting Help with Your Proofreading

The problem with proofreading your own book is this: you're too close to the book, and you're going to see what you want to see. You'll read a sentence you've looked at many times before, and your eyes will play tricks on you – you'll completely miss the fact that you've repeated the word *the* twice in a row, or you've written *than* instead of *that*. With careful reading, you'll hopefully spot lots of mistakes, but you're unlikely to spot them all.

Ask a friend or a family member or a colleague to proofread your book and you may be surprised at what he spots.

Even better, hire a professional proofreader. An experienced, trained proofreader will see the mistakes and inconsistencies that you've missed, and will make all sorts of corrections in your book that you wouldn't know to make.

My clients are often staggered by the number of corrections I make in a book that they thought was just about ready to publish.

'Good grief!' they say. 'And here was I thinking that I was a pretty good writer...'

'Don't worry about it,' is my response. '*Every* writer needs a proofreader. The books you buy in the shops by bestselling authors? They've all been proofread. The books you read by the most amazing authors? They've all been proofread. I've proofread many books for publishers and authors, and I know just how many mistakes authors make. It's okay – you don't *have* to know every nook and cranny of the English language. Your job is to write; a proofreader's job is to proofread.'

Improving Your Proofreading Skills

Just because I advise you to have your book proofread, that doesn't mean you shouldn't proofread it yourself. Many times.

The more you proofread, the more mistakes you find. And the more mistakes you find, the fewer mistakes are left in the book. Which means whoever else you ask to proofread your book has fewer mistakes to spot, which makes his job easier (and, if you're hiring a proofreader, it lowers the cost).

And the better you become at proofreading over time, the less proofreading support you need. You always need to have someone else proofread your book, to spot the stuff that's in your blind spot, but eventually that proofreader is only spotting a handful of mistakes.

Tips for Effective Proofreading

Here's some guidance on how best to proofread:
• Read after a break. Don't expect to proofread a chapter of your book right after you finish writing it – you're too close to see inconsistencies and errors. By all means give it a quick scan, but then put it away and come back to it.

- Read somewhere quiet. Proofreading on the bus or in a cafe isn't ideal because you're surrounded by distractions. Try to read when and where you can really focus on the book.

- Read slowly. Speed-reading doesn't make for effective proofreading. Slow. Right. Down. Yes, it's irritating plodding through the text, but by looking carefully at each word you're much more likely to spot issues.

- Read aloud. If you can bear the sound of your voice droning in an echoey room, read aloud. You notice so many more issues this way.

- Format for easy reading. Use an easy-to-read font at 12-point size. Double-space, and use wide margins.

- Read on paper. Print your book out – you notice problems on paper that you've completely missed on-screen.

- Keep a good dictionary to hand. If in doubt, look it up!

- Read at least twice. Try to leave a gap between each read of at least a few days.

Word to the Wise: Don't expect your spellchecker to do the job of proofreading. Spellcheckers and grammar-checkers are great for weeding out the odd typo and double space between two words, but they have serious limitations when it comes to top-notch proofreading. For example, my spellchecker had no problem with this sentence: *The companies what make spell-cheques no that it is a use full tool but that it does knot guarantee miss-take-free writing.* And do bear in mind that most spellcheckers are set to US English, so will correct inaccurately for UK English.

What to Look for When You Proofread

Part 4 helps you hone your writing skills, so your language is in pretty good shape. And you should have already stripped out most of the mistakes in your book at the editing stage. So what you're looking for when you proofread are those odd bits and bobs that you've missed during your many read-throughs of the book before now.

Here are some of the issues to look for that may have crept through your eagle-eyed editing:

Spelling:
- Mistakes – obvious typos should leap out; but take care where you've simply used the wrong word (for example, the previous sentence may read: *obvious types should leaf out; but take care were you're simply use the wrong work*).
- Inconsistencies – for example, *organise* on one page, *organize* on the next.

Punctuation:
- Mistakes – for example, stray commas, missing full stops, speech marks in the wrong place or facing the wrong way, hyphens that should be dashes, incorrect use of colons or semi-colons and too many dots in an ellipsis.
- Inconsistencies – for example, serial comma is used in some places, but not others; ellipses are styled differently.

Grammar:
- Subject and verb don't agree – for example, *A set of books are available* (should be *A set... is available*).

- Tense shifts – for example, *He went to the window and looks out.*
- Incorrect verb conjugation – for example, *I was sat on the bed.*

Style:
- Incorrect or inconsistent capitalisation – for example, *My Mum is amazing* and *WHat a mess*. Also look carefully for the number *1* and the lower case *l* masquerading as an *I*.
- Incorrect or inconsistent italicisation – for example, 'My favourite book is *Great* Expectations and I also love *Oliver Twist*.'
- Incorrect or inconsistent number style – for example, *At the shop I bought three oranges and 5 bananas.*

Accuracy:
- Facts are wrong – for example, *That afternoon we went to Hyde Park in Chiswick, London.*
- You haven't said what you meant to say – for example, *She was happy to discover that her hair had fallen out*, when you mean, *She was not happy to discover that her hair had fallen out.*

Format and layout:
- Font is inconsistent – you shift between multiple fonts and font sizes.
- Spacing is inconsistent – for example, you move from double spacing to single spacing.
- Indenting is inconsistent – for example, some paragraphs are indented on the first line, but others aren't.

- Headings are inconsistent – for example, Some Are in Initial Caps, Like This, and some are IN ALL CAPS, LIKE THIS.
- Random formatting has crept in – for example, a paragraph is bold, or right-justified, or underlined.

Try This: If you spot a really awful mistake (*pubic* places instead of *public*, or lunch in a *brassiere* rather than a *brasserie*), do a global search for the mistake to check it doesn't exist anywhere else in the book.

In a Nutshell

- Care about the standard of your book – develop, edit and proofread to ensure the book is as good as it can be.
- Be open to the idea of professional support.
- Allow some time to elapse between finishing the book and polishing it.
- Be your own critic.
- Look at all aspects of your book and develop them as far as possible.
- Check and tidy the language.
- Know when it's time to put the red pen away and move on.
- Ask other people's opinions on your book – but make sure you're getting honest feedback.
- Develop your book afresh following feedback.
- Proofread your book carefully several times.
- Ask at least one other person – ideally a professional – to proofread the book too.

16. Publishing Your Book

You've written the book and you've polished it up. Now comes the stage you're most excited about: publishing it so that the world can read your fabulous book and you can put it on your bookshelf and gaze at it with pride.

This chapter helps you understand your options: trying to get published or publishing the book yourself.

Choosing Between Traditional Publishing and Self-publishing

You probably already have an idea of which path you intend to take, but now's the time to firm up your plans. The following sections help you see the pros and cons of the choices, to help you decide which is the best fit for you.

GETTING PUBLISHED

Traditional publishing means:

- A publisher publishes your book.
- You don't pay a penny for the publisher to publish your book.
- The publisher pays you a royalty per copy sold (and sometimes an advance on the royalty).

- The publisher takes care of editing, proofreading, typesetting, design, publication and some marketing.
- You do some marketing too. (See Chapter 17.)

Pros:
- Books published by publishers are respected by authors.
- The publisher has a wealth of expertise to apply to developing your book and marketing it well.
- The publisher supports you in all aspects of the publishing process.
- The publisher may be prepared to put more money into marketing your book than you are.
- You're more likely to have bookshops stock your book.
- You may sell more copies than via self-publishing.
- You get the confidence boost that comes with having been signed by a publisher – it improves your credibility as an author.

Cons:
- Only a small proportion of authors who submit their books get a publishing contract.
- You don't retain full control over your book – although most publishers do their best to accommodate authors' wishes, you may have to accept editing and design and marketing decisions you don't entirely agree with.
- It takes a while to be published even once you're signed – from six to eighteen months.
- You might not make as much money per copy sold as you would through self-publishing.

- Traditional publishing is for books that are highly marketable and exceptionally good.

SELF-PUBLISHING

Self-publishing means:

- You publish your book, either all on your own or with the help of a self-publishing company.
- You pay all the costs associated with publishing your book.*
- You receive all the proceeds from book sales, after costs.
- You either have a self-publishing company take care of aspects like editing, proofreading, typesetting, design and publication, or you source your own professionals to provide these services.
- You do all the marketing (the self-publishing company may help to a degree).

Pros:

- There are no rejections – you're free to publish.
- You keep full control of your book – you can publish it just as you like.
- You may make more money per copy sold than you would through traditional publishing.
- You can publish quickly.

---

* Some publishers also offer partnership publishing, where you both invest in the book.

Cons:

- Self-publishing is increasingly respected; but there are still some who let the side down with shoddy books, and you may encounter the odd snob who doesn't see the merits of your self-published book.
- Books published by publishers are most respected by authors.
- You're less likely to have bookshops stock your book.
- You may not sell as many copies as you would if you were traditionally published.
- You have to do it all yourself – which is a lot of work, and you'll have plenty to learn.
- You have to invest your money in the book – so you have to sell a good number of books to recoup your investment, and even more books to have reached the point where the profit is above that which you'd have earned through traditional publishing.
- Self-publishing is for books that are marketable, though perhaps not to a massive or proven market, and exceptionally good, or really good but not quite grabbing a publisher.

Submitting to Agents/Publishers

If you've decided you want to submit your book to agents and/or publishers, I encourage you to look back at Chapter 2 to make sure you understand the agent/publisher's perspective. Then work through the following sections, which will get you submitting.

AGENT OR PUBLISHER?

Some publishers are open to submissions direct from authors; many – especially the big ones – only look at books sent by literary agents.

Whether you need an agent depends a lot on the book you've written. You can often submit non-fiction proposals directly to the publisher. Unless your non-fiction book is going to be mass market – for example, you're an expert in the field and there's a huge market for the book – I wouldn't advise taking it to an agent. If the most your book will make is a couple of grand in royalties, the agent's cut will be paltry, so it's not worth the agent's while helping you place the book with a publisher.

Fiction, however, often does merit having an agent. It really depends on your aspirations. If you've written a techno thriller that you know is pretty good but isn't something a big publisher would take, and you know a small independent publisher that specialises in techno thrillers and is open to submissions, you'll probably go straight to that publisher. On the other hand, if you've written a novel that you believe is mass market and could be a great commercial success, you want a chance of having a big publisher take your book on – and that means getting an agent.

RESEARCHING AGENTS/PUBLISHERS

Most authors make the mistake of finalising the submission

package (see the next section) before working out which publishers/agents they're targeting.

Agents and publishers don't appreciate receiving blanket submissions – where it's clear you haven't read their submission instructions and you've sent the same letter to several other agents/publishers at the same time. Worse still is when you haven't bothered to look at their websites to check they're actually interested in the kind of book you've written.

Word to the Wise: Never try to convert a publisher/agent. Letters that begin *I notice on your website you don't publish science fiction, but my book is really rather special, so I thought I'd give you a try in case you were prepared to make an exception…* are maddening to agents/publishers!

Research all agents and publishers carefully. Do a web search, and use writers' guides – in the UK the *Writers' and Artists' Yearbook* is your bible for details of agents/publishers.

Toolkit: Draw up a list of agents and publishers who are open to submissions and interested in your kind of book. Prioritise the list – put those you like best at the top.

PUTTING TOGETHER THE SUBMISSION PACKAGE

For fiction books, a submission package usually consists of a covering letter, a synopsis (outline of the book) and the first three chapters. For non-fiction books, the submission package will be the same, but it may also include a chapter breakdown and some detailed information on the market and your marketing ideas.

The good news is, you've already done a lot of the work required for your submission package. You've written the book; you've put together a synopsis and a chapter outline; and you've worked out the essential elements of the covering letter: the genre, the target reader and the USP (see Chapter 4). Now you need to shape up the synopsis and covering letter, and then adapt them according to each publisher/agent's rules for submission.

Remember: Your submission must be tailored to meet the requirements of the individual agent/publisher to which you're submitting. This is really, really important. If the agent asks for the first 10,000 words, that's what you send. If the publisher asks you to double-space the submission materials, that's what you do.

It sounds obvious, I know, but countless authors fail to do as they're asked. By not following the rules, you show a lack of professionalism and an inability to follow instructions – not attractive qualities in an author. You also annoy the reader for the agent/publisher. And an annoyed reader is going to struggle to engage with your book.

Here are some general guidelines for your submission package (but do remember to check the rules of the agent/publisher):

- Covering letter: Keep it to one side of A4. Address it to the right person – not just *Dear Sir/Madam*. Include the title of the book, the genre, the target reader and the USP. Explain the basic story of the book (one paragraph maximum). Explain a little about yourself, especially details that are marketable and noteworthy writing experience.

- Synopsis: I usually recommend that my clients write a short synopsis (one side of A4) and a longer, more detailed one – send whichever fits the agent/publisher's requirements. Introduce the theme, the central character(s) and the setting. Outline the key events. Summarise your book in such a way that the reader understands what it's all about, and wants to read it. Use the present tense, third person and write in a straightforward manner – this isn't a blurb or a sales pitch. No cliffhangers – tell the agent/publisher exactly what the story is.

- First three chapters: Make sure it is the first three chapters you submit if that's what the agent/publisher requests. If you have a short introduction or prologue you can include that; if these are long, they act as a first chapter. Don't include a random selection of chapters – agents/publishers want to see the start of the book, to see whether you grab the reader's interest. If you don't think the start of the book is strong enough to submit, rewrite it!

Remember: Once you've finished putting together the submission, proofread it carefully.

SENDING OUT YOUR BOOK

If you're going to approach agents, do that first before sending the book to publishers that are open to submission. If you get nowhere with agents, then work through publishers.

Follow the instructions on the agent/publisher's website for submission. If they prefer postal submissions, print the book and include an SAE if you want it back. You can also include an SAE acknowledgement that they have received it. Alternatively, email the book over with your covering letter in the body of the email and your synopsis and chapters as attachments.

The traditional advice is that you only send out one or two submissions at a time. But given that many agents/publishers take weeks – months, even – to reply, that approach is slow and torturous. My advice is to send the book out to a handful at a time, and have a rolling schedule so that you send out a batch every month.

Remember: Keep track of which agents/publishers you've submitted to! Otherwise you may get confused and forget a few or double up submissions.

Some agents/publishers respond quickly. Some take their time. Don't hound them. They hate that.

Word to the Wise: If an agent/publisher likes your book, their first question is often, 'Who else have you sent this to?' Be honest. It's a great sign that the agent/publisher is anxious about where else your book has gone; don't annoy them now by lying in the hope that you can play them off against another agent/publisher.

Chapter 18 helps you decide next steps when you've either got a publishing contract or not had any interest from agents/publishers.

Being Your Own Publisher

There's a reason I've called this section 'Being Your Own Publisher' – that's exactly what self-publishing is. Think, for a moment, about all the jobs a publisher does. If you self-publish, as well as doing all the jobs an author does, you need to do all those that a publisher does as well. It's a lot of work, but it's mightily empowering and can be very fulfilling.

GOING IT ALONE

Not for the faint-hearted, but I have had clients who've set up their own publishing companies. Be aware that this is a big undertaking that requires investment and a lot of hard graft, and it's probably only worth it if you intend to publish lots of books, or other people's books as well as your own.

USING A SELF-PUBLISHING COMPANY

A self-publishing company takes care of some of the business side of publishing for you. For example, Matador, a division of Troubador Publishing (the publisher of this book), offers a self-publishing service that includes everything you need to get the book in print and in ebook format and up for sale on major book-retailing websites and in bookshops.

Increasingly, some authors are abandoning print books entirely and going straight to ebook format. Amazon self-publishing is especially popular – due to some inspiring success stories of authors who've done very well.

Whatever self-publishing service provider you choose, research it carefully to be sure it is well-established, commercially aware and has a good reputation in the industry. Matador, for example, has been recommended in the *Writers' and Artists' Yearbook*, the UK publishing bible, for five consecutive years.

Word to the Wise: Beware small, inexperienced self-publishing providers and those who are clearly taking advantage of authors. Look for a good number of titles published, some impressive results from people who've self-published with them and clear information about the company. Most of all, look at the books published. Do they look decent? Are the covers good?

Quality is Key: Getting Professionals on Board

Whether you self-publish all by yourself or through a self-publishing company, if you want to publish a marketable book, you're best using some professional services.

The biggest complaint readers make about self-published books is that they're amateur – not of a professional standard. You can commission for yourself publishing professionals to help you create a quality book:

- Editor/proofreader
- Typesetter
- Cover designer

Some self-publishing companies offer these services as part of the self-publishing package. Great – just make sure you check the quality of the services. If you're not 100 per cent sure that the designer or editor is highly experienced and skilled, find your own.

THE PRICE IS RIGHT?

Price is a big factor that determines whether a reader buys your book.

Ebooks

For ebooks, you've a choice: the Wallmart approach (stack 'em high, sell 'em cheap) or the Waitrose approach (reassuringly expensive). It really depends on how you want to pitch yourself in the market. Pricing should form part of your marketing strategy (see Chapter 17). The best approach is to have a good look at the cost of ebooks on Amazon, and check out the prices of competing self-published titles.

MB example: Kerry Wilkinson

In March 2012 *The Telegraph* reported that self-published author Kerry Wilkinson had signed a six-book deal with Pan MacMillan. Across his three books, *Locked In*, *Vigilante* and *Woman in Black*, Wilkinson sold 250,000 copies in six months. Part of his success comes down to pricing the first novel, *Locked In*, at 99p to attract readers.

Print Books

Print books are tricky. A lot of self-publishing these days is based on print-on-demand – so the book is printed when the reader buys it, and then sent out. The cost per book tends to be quite high. I've seen self-published authors cost a novel at £15.00, and it just doesn't sell well.

The lower you can get the price of the book and still make a decent profit, the better. You may decide to have a print run of the book – say 1,000 copies. The larger the print run, the lower the production cost per book. But the larger the print run, the higher the risk of having unsold books that you lose money on.

It's really up to you to decide how marketable your book is. If you've created a great book and you intend to pull out all the stops with marketing (see Chapter 17), you may be best having a print run. If you're not at all sure that your book will do well, but you're keen to self-publish it, you either have to swallow having a high price (and realise that this in itself deters readers) or perhaps remove the risk of losing money and publish it to ebook format to start off with.

Entering Competitions

Another route to publication is via a competition. A handful of competitions for authors exist whose prize is publication or a sum of money you can put towards self-publishing.

I'm the founder of The Novel Prize for unpublished novelists, which is a platform for exploring serious self-publishing. (For details, visit www.thebookspecialist.com.) Other prizes also exist; some focus on a particular genre. Spend some time surfing the internet to see which competitions are upcoming or open for entries.

The downside of entering competitions is that you're up against a host of other authors, and you usually have to wait some time before the winner is announced. The reward if you win, however, is great in terms of publishing a marketable book – because prize-winners are highly marketable.

In a Nutshell

- Traditional publishing is for books that are highly marketable and exceptionally good.
- Self-publishing is for books that are marketable and exceptionally good, or really good.
- If you've written a non-fiction book or a novel for a small market, take it straight to publishers.
- If you've written a novel and you've big aspirations for it, submit it to agents.
- Research agents/publishers meticulously.
- Tailor each submission to meet the requirements of the individual agent/publisher to which you're submitting.
- Send out submissions in batches, and keep a log.
- Check out a self-publishing company's credentials carefully.
- Ensure a quality product by using professionals.
- Give plenty of thought to book pricing, and keep it as low as you can.
- Look into competitions that you can enter with your book.

17. Marketing Your Book

It's beyond the scope of this book to give you detailed information on book marketing – it's a topic so wide it merits a book of its own. But no book on writing a book that can be successfully marketed is complete without some consideration of how you market a book: how you tell readers about your book and encourage them to buy it.

This chapter gives you an overview of book marketing that you can use to inform your writing and help you to drive sales post-publication.

For a more detailed look at book marketing, I recommend *A Seriously Useful Author's Guide to Marketing and Publicising Books* by Mary Cavanagh (published by Troubador). I'm also in the process of writing a guide to online marketing for authors; check my website www.thebookspecialist.com for details.

Why Market?

Because if you don't, you won't sell many (if any) books. There's no point writing an amazing book if no one knows it exists.

If you self-publish, you are entirely responsible for marketing. If you don't market your book, you're not really publishing it – you're just printing it.

If you get published the traditional way, you get some support from the publisher — but you still need to do plenty of marketing yourself if you want your book to sell well.

Working Hard

Marketing is a big job. If you want to be a full-time writer, at some point that job will involve partly writing and partly marketing your writing. If you want a marketable book — a book that sells — you have to put in a lot of effort beyond the writing stage.

I've seen fabulous books published that flop simply because the author isn't prepared to put in the hours to get that book noticed, and read.

MB example: *Eragon* by Christopher Paolini

Christopher Paolini was just 15 when he started writing his first novel, *Eragon*. His parents self-published it, and set up book signings in bookshops, libraries and schools across the USA — 135 in total. As a result, *Eragon* caught the attention of publishing house Alfred A. Knopf, which offered Paolini a contract. Fast-forward a decade and Paolini has published three more books, to complete the Inheritance Cycle series, and *Eragon* is a major feature film. Through putting in the hours in marketing his first book, Paolini created his own success.

Considering Cost

Many authors assume that book marketing is expensive. It certainly can be – if you're putting ads in *The Bookseller* and on the walls of Tube stations, and having a swanky launch party in The Ivy. But you can also market a book very inexpensively simply by putting in hard work with promotion and online marketing. I've got clients who've done well getting their books noticed without shelling out more than a few hundred pounds on a website, a spot of consultancy (that helped them know how to market) and some promotional materials.

When it comes to book marketing, effort often counts more than spend. Thirty hours spent on free social media marketing will likely create more interest in your book than paying your local bookshop to place the book in its window for a week.

Toolkit: Decide on a marketing budget. Be realistic about what that will buy you – do your research. Make the budget as big as possible, and then make it stretch as far as you can.

Marketing Your Book, and Yourself

In Chapter 2, I explain the importance of being a marketable author. Once you've published your book, you aren't just marketing the book – you're also marketing yourself as its author.

Breaking Down Marketing

If you are published by a traditional publisher, there are three levels to marketing:

* The book
* The brand under which it's published (e.g. Hodder Headline)
* You as author

If you self-publish, there are two levels to marketing:

* The book
* You as author

You, as author, are a brand of sorts – by which I mean you have an identity when it comes to marketing.

Publishing is an unusual business in this sense; not many businesses expect the creator of a product to have so much involvement in marketing. Say you invent a new kind of nappy for babies – one that never, ever, ever leaks (oh, how parents will love that!). The marketing strategy is all about the product. You don't expect anyone to be remotely interested in you, the creator – although the consumer is probably interested in the brand you establish, No-Leak Nappies, under which you market the product.

Remember: Readers want to know about you, the author. All marketing involves telling people about you, as well as telling people about your book.

Thinking About Your Profile as an Author

Having established that readers are going to want to know about you as an author, think about the image you want to project.

- Open about your life – to a point: You want readers to know a little about your personal life, but not too much. So you might be clear that you live in Windsor, have a job cleaning the Queen's fish tanks, have a wife and three kids, and have a passion for Cliff Richard songs.

- Friendly to readers: You want readers to feel that you're a nice, approachable person who's delighted and grateful that they've bought your book.

- Fun: When it comes to marketing, a sense of humour really helps. You want people to like you. Making them smile is a good start.

- Serious about your book: You want to appear professional and capable – at the level of bestselling authors.

What you *don't* want is to come across as rude or aggressive or stuck-up or amateur or boring or aloof or suspiciously tight-lipped about who you are. But neither do you want to share too much about your life. Readers don't want to know you intimately. They don't want to hear about your in-growing toenail; or your grief over the death of Fluffy, your cat; or your row with your partner; or that time you were so blind drunk you climbed a tree in a toga. That's just unprofessional.

Word to the Wise: Be very careful what's written about you, or by you, online. Say a bloke called Zebedee Zingbot (a pretty unusual name) publishes a historical romance novel. He's already got a personal Twitter account, a Facebook account and a blog in that name in which he mouths off about his ex-girlfriend and posts rude 'jokes' that are derogatory to women. Pretty quickly, readers marry up Zebedee Zingbot the historical romance novelist, and Zebedee Zingbot the woman-hater. Not ideal for book sales. Zebedee would have been better either pulling down all the web content that's damaging to his reputation as a novelist, or publishing under a pen name (see the following section).

Try This: Split your social media activities into business and personal – so set up separate Facebook and Twitter and blogging accounts.

MB example: Louise Voss and Mark Edwards

Louise Voss and Mark Edwards, co-authors of the books *Killing Cupid* and *Catch Your Death*, were the first UK indie authors to reach the number one spot in both the Amazon Kindle and Amazon Fiction charts. Their profile as co-authors has been carefully considered and built. Take a look at their website at http://vossandedwards.com. It's a well-designed site that successfully markets both the books and the authors. You can find out about the authors, feel part of a community of their readers (you may even be Reader of the Month) and – crucially – contact Mark and Louise.

A NOTE ON PSEUDONYMS

A pseudonym is a pen name – a name you use for your publishing. Here are some reasons you may choose to use a pseudonym for your book:

- If you've an unusual name you need to disassociate from: See the Zebedee Zingbot example in the previous section.
- If confidentiality is an issue: For example, you've written a memoir in which you talk about being abused, and want to protect those involved. (Confidentiality issues pull in potential libel issues – check carefully that nothing you're writing can get you in hot water.)
- If you hate your own name, and think it gives the wrong image: For example, your name is Prunella Poo, or She-tee Writer.
- If your book would in some way damage your business/personal reputation: For example, you're a high-powered banker and you've written an erotic novel.
- If you need to create a separate persona for writing in this genre, because you already write quite differently in another genre: For example, *Guardian* journalist Jonathan Freedland writes thrillers under the pen name Sam Bourne.
- If you've created a book whose entire concept relies on the pseudonym: For example, your book may be narrated by a character you devise, and published under that character's name – like my novelette *Publish or Perish* by Sue Dunim.
- If you're on the run and need to keep your identity

under wraps: Possibly I've been reading too many thrillers.

Before getting carried away coming up with a name – and that really is the fun part! – give some thought to marketability. You'll need to be able to successfully market the book under this pen name. If you're writing under a pseudonym because you're trying to protect your privacy, you may struggle to really engage with marketing because you're holding yourself back. Publishers in particular aren't enamoured with pen names for the very reason that they know marketing can be more challenging.

UMB example: If I told you, I'd have to kill you

You're a nanny for a member of the royal family. You've signed a confidentiality agreement with the family. In your book, you 'expose' all sorts of shenanigans that go on behind closed doors. To protect identities, you change all names, locations, dates and most of the facts in the book, and you publish it under a pen name. In fact, the book has become an exposé by a major politician's gardener – both politician and gardener unnamed.

Word to the Wise: If you do write under a pen name, take care to use it when required. I have a pen name, and I quite often sign an email that should have gone out under that name with Charlie Wilson, greatly confusing the recipient. And I have to work quite hard to remember my 'name' when addressed on the phone or at an event.

Getting Your Book into the Shops

If you've self-published, or published with a small publisher, into print, you may need to do a little work to get your book into shops. Unless your book has huge appeal, you're going to struggle to get every branch of Waterstones (I hate not using an apostrophe) to stock it. But local bookshops are often very supportive of local authors. For example, my closest bookshop (Waterstones [grrr!] in Nottingham) has a large local interest section right beside the main tills which features books from local authors. Send an email to the manager – or better yet, go into the shop in person so that the staff can see you're a nice, professional, sane author – and ask whether the shop will stock, and promote, the book. You may even be allowed to hold a book-signing event.

Remember: Do be aware that publishers pay lots of money to have a book on the chart bookshelves at the front of the store and laid out on tables. Unless you've a huge budget, such high-level marketing is out of your reach.

Offline Marketing

Offline marketing covers all the marketing activities you can do that don't involve the internet:

- Advertising: You pay to advertise your book – for example, in papers and magazines, on posters or billboards, or on inserts in a magazine or product marketed to authors. My advice: steer clear of advertising. It's expensive. And I think someone is more likely to buy your book if it's talked about in a magazine, rather than advertised there. Put your energy into PR (getting your book talked about for free) instead.

- Articles in magazines and newspapers: Excellent publicity, if you can come up with an article related to your book that an editor will want.

- Book launch: You have a nice party to celebrate the publication of your book. It's only really worth doing if you think you can get a decent number of attendees – and attract some publicity from the launch.

- Book placement: Your local bookshop may be happy to stock your title. Or you may talk your local health spa into having a few copies of your *Total Relaxation* book. If you can't actually place the books – because it's tricky for non-book retailers to sell books – try to place some marketing materials; for example, a flyer advertising your sci-fi novel on the counter of your local Monsters and Mayhem comic book store.

- Book signings: You sit at a table in your local bookshop with a stack of your books. You either have a queue of people wanting to buy a signed copy of your book (if so, you've done really well), or you spend the day charming visitors to the bookshop into buying your book.

- Endorsements: Seek endorsements from suitably expert and/or well-known people. But do make sure they're relevant to your book. For example, a nice quote from Katie Price about your book *Boobalicious: In Celebration of the Boob Job* is relevant, if you can get it. Praise from friend-of-a-friend Noel Edmunds for your fantasy horror novel isn't much good. And while it's super to get really high-profile people endorsing the book, also consider less famous sorts. For example, 'Every accountant should read this book' by Accountingweb.com is a useful endorsement for your book *What You May Not Realise About Taxation Laws*.

- Radio: Often overlooked, but a great way to get people talking about your book. In particular, check out your local radio stations – they're often interested in a local author.

- Reader competition: A great way to generate publicity. It may be as simple as a book giveaway, or you may offer some kind of launch goody. For example, *To celebrate the launch of my new book,* The Ghosts of Waverley Manor, *I'm giving one lucky reader the chance to win a night for two in Waverley Manor, the most haunted building in England. To enter, do xyz.* (**Word to the Wise:** If running a competition, make sure you've toed the line when it comes to the Gambling Commission's rules; see: www.gamblingcommission.gov.uk.)

- Reviews in press: Send out free copies to book reviewers and ask for reviews. But do be aware that if you solicit reviews, you have to accept that the reviewers will give their honest opinions!

- Speaking engagements: Perhaps give a talk at a local school or college, or at your local library. If you've written something literary that's got good reviews, also check out literary festivals – there are lots in the UK, ranging from a low-key event on a village green up to a massive one like Edinburgh.

- Television: Unlikely to pan out (pardon the pun) for most authors, but if you spot an opportunity, grab it.

Try This: If you're struggling with offline marketing, consider hiring a publicist. Do a Google search, and look for one who's friendly and professional and has an impressive track record.

Online Marketing

Online marketing, also known as digital marketing, is a key area for book marketing. It's really effective – readers these days respond very well to online marketing. Here are some ideas:

- Author profiles: Look where your book is for sale online, and see which websites allow you to set up an author profile. As a minimum, set up profiles on Amazon and Goodreads.
- Blogging: You're a writer, so it makes sense that you use writing to promote your book. Write a blog that relates to your book, and also look for opportunities to guest blog (where you blog on someone else's blog).
- Book groups: All sorts of book groups exist online. Have a browse and see whether any relate to your genre.
- Facebook: Set up an account you'll use for your author stuff, and a page for your book. Then post comments, links, pictures, news and so on.
- Other social media: Keep an eye on what's up-and-coming in social media – it's moving at a breathtaking pace. For example, at the time of writing I've been getting into Pinterest, a kind of visual Twitter.
- Rich media: Videos, book trailers, podcasts – there are

lots of creative angles you can explore with other types of media.

- Twitter: A great medium for book promotion. You can use it to learn more about publishing, to run competitions, to share news and to build a strong following of readers who like you, and like your writing.
- Website: If you're serious about marketing your book, you need a website. It needn't be Flash (techie readers will get that pun), and nor does it have to cost much. But get something online so readers have a place to come to find out more about you and connect with you (yes, I advise having an email address – be friendly!).

Try This: Digital marketing is a vast and fast-changing area. Try to keep up to date with current trends, and if you're struggling, get some support.

Being Creative with Marketing

Many authors get hot and sweaty at the thought of marketing. Because it sounds so corporate, and because it calls to mind cheesy promotion or aggressive selling.

But marketing, in fact, can be a lot of fun – and an opportunity to be creative. You could:

- Do a publicity stunt – for example, if you've written a history of Heinz, sit in a bath of baked beans outside its factory.
- Form your own fan club.

- Get your book cover printed onto a t-shirt and wear it everywhere.
- Stick a book cover transfer on your car.
- Hold a book reading in a local cafe.
- Stage a scene from your book and put it up on YouTube.
- Offer some fun extra materials on your website, such as an alternative ending or an additional chapter.
- Ask all your local shops to support you.
- Print a flyer/business card with your book details and leave the odd one about – e.g. on a restaurant table after you pay the bill or on the Tube. (Just one at a time, mind; don't get in trouble for illegal leafleting.)
- Forget Santa and snowy landscapes; stick your book cover on your Christmas cards.

I could go on, and on, but you get the idea. Have fun with it!

My favourite thing about marketing? You get to meet lots of new people. And for a writer, whose job is solitary and pretty lonely, that's great.

MB example: *The Seven Year Bitch* by Jennifer Belle

When the independent publicist that Jennifer Belle's publisher hired to promote her book *The Seven Year Bitch* got no results, Jennifer decided to take matters into her own hands. She hired an actress to read her book aloud on the New York subway and at major landmarks for $8 per hour. The result: the *New York Times* and the *New York Post* picked up the story.

Devising a Marketing Programme

Having given some thought to your profile as an author and the many avenues you can explore in marketing the book, now sit down and put together a marketing programme.

Toolkit: Make a plan, outlining the marketing activities you intend to carry out. Note down:

- Whether you can do them alone, or need support
- The cost, if any
- The estimated time required

Then put the list in order, with the most important activities at the top.

Try This: The best approach is to set aside a chunk of time each week to devote to marketing. If you set up a blog, you're bound to struggle to put up posts regularly – unless you schedule in time to write the entries.

In a Nutshell

- You need to market your book so people know it exists.
- Whether you self-publish or traditionally publish, you've got to get involved with marketing.
- You need to commit time to marketing; it's a big job.
- Come up with a marketing budget and spend it wisely.
- Readers want to know about you, the author, as well as your book.

- Think about how you come across to your readers – be friendly and professional.
- Select which elements of your personal life you share carefully.
- If using a pseudonym, think about how that affects marketability.
- Market offline.
- Market online.
- Market as much as you can.
- Have fun with marketing.
- Set down a strategy and schedule, and stick to them.

18. When the Dust Settles: Post-Submission/Publication

You've done it! You've found The Idea, you've planned the book, you've written the book, you've polished the book and you've either published the book or had a good stab at it.

Now what?

This concise, final chapter helps you decide your next steps – whether you're going back to the drawing board or back to the day job.

Assessing the Success of Your Book

Time to take a serious look at your book. How well has it done?

IF YOU APPROACHED AGENTS/PUBLISHERS...

Here are your measures of success.

Your book hasn't done well if:
- No one was interested in your book.
- You received some negative feedback from agents/publishers.

Your book has done pretty well, and has potential, if:

- You got some positive feedback from agents/publishers, but they didn't want the book.
- An agent/publisher asked you for the full manuscript, but didn't take it further.

Your book has done really well, and has potential, if:

- An agent/publisher asked you to revise the book in line with their suggestions, but didn't sign you.
- An agent signed you, but couldn't get a publisher interested.

Your book has done brilliantly if:

- You got a publisher.

If you approached agents/publishers, you no doubt wanted the book to be brilliantly successful and get published. But doing pretty well or really well isn't too shabby either – you may have the makings of a book you can develop to a standard that will hook a publisher, or you may have the next self-publishing sensation on your hands.

IF YOU SELF-PUBLISHED...

Here are your measures of success.

Your book hasn't done well if:

- No one has bought your book other than your mum, your wife and you.

- You've got many gut-wrenchingly terrible reviews, such as *I'd rather stick needles in my eyes than read another book by this author* and *The worst book I've ever read. Ever. DO NOT BUY THIS BOOK.*
- No one wants to publicise the book.
- Your book has become an example of a terrible book held up for others to ridicule.

Your book has done pretty well if:
- You've sold 100 copies to people you *don't* know.
- You've got some positive reviews.
- You've had some limited publicity.

Your book has done really well if:
- You've sold hundreds of copies.
- You've had lots of good reviews.
- You've had some good publicity.

Your book has done brilliantly if:
- You've sold thousands of copies.
- You've got loads of great reviews.
- There's a buzz about your book – people are recommending it, praising it, excited by it.
- Your book has become an example of great self-publishing.
- You're being pestered to write the next book.

For your first book, doing pretty well is commendable indeed. Self-published authors have gone on to achieve super sales with later books based on done-pretty-well first books. Really well and above; well, that's exciting stuff. Brilliantly well – hooray, you're living the dream!

Moving Forward When You Want to Get Published

If you've sent the book out to agents/publishers and it hasn't done as well as you'd like, you have a choice: put it away, develop it further or self-publish it.

First, work out what's held an agent/publisher back from taking on your book:

- Your book isn't great. It's too long, it's confusing, it's offensive, it doesn't make sense – you've ignored all the advice in this book.
- Your book isn't marketable. It's a 500,000-word history of LED lights. You're not quite sure who'd want to read it, but you love LED lights. Oh dear. Did you read this book before writing yours?
- Your covering letter, synopsis and first three chapters have let you down. You've fallen at the first hurdle because the agents/publishers weren't grabbed by your submission.
- Your book is good, but it's not exceptional. A common problem. An agent or publisher has to adore your book before giving you a contract to sign. Not just like it. Or even love it. *Adore* it. Many good books don't get published. (See Chapter 2 for more on this topic.)

If you're at the end of the road with agents/publishers, you need to decide where to go from here:

- Self-publish your book. If you're confident that your book is good, self-publishing is a viable option. Not sure whether it's good? Get an expert opinion, or go through this book closely to see whether your book ticks the boxes. For more on self-publishing, head to Chapter 16.
- Give up on the book, and on writing. Take a look at the later section 'Throwing in the Towel?'.
- Give up on the book, and write another. Take a look at the later section 'Writing the Next Book'.

If you do decide to give up on the book, don't bin it – just put it away for now. In later years you'll appreciate being able to look back on this, your first book. And you never know – the world may not be ready for *Marjory MacMarvel's Magical Mammaries* just now, but we may be in a few years.

Moving Forward When You've Self-published

If you've self-published your book and the response and sales have been disappointing, try to identify what's gone wrong. It's likely to be one of the following:

- Your book isn't great. It's boring, it's silly, it's poorly written – you've ignored all the advice in this book.
- Your book isn't marketable. It's an autobiography of your life, and you've done nothing more exciting in the past 30 years than decorate your spare room. There's no market for the book. Oh dear. Did you read this book before writing yours?
- Your book isn't marketed well. A very common problem –

no one knows the book exists! You've put it up on Amazon and then sat back expecting the pounds to pile in.

- Your book isn't professionally published. You've formatted the ebook yourself and made a pig's ear of it – the text is all over the shop. Or you've used a shoddy self-publishing company that's made you a cover a five-year-old could draw and printed it on wafer-thin paper. Or you've made the cover yourself in Microsoft Paint and printed it yourself on your inkjet.
- Your book is too expensive. You're asking the reader to pay £14.99 for a paperback novel.

If you need to step up your marketing, get a new cover or drop the price, go for it – it can't hurt. But if you've realised that the book is seriously flawed, you've a harder decision to make about where to go from here. You can either:

- Redevelop the book and have another stab at self-publishing. If no one really noticed you publish the book, you can get away with having another go at developing it. Just be sure that the book has potential – if you've followed all the guidance in this book, you've a good starting point; if you've been speed-reading this book and ignoring the advice, there may be nothing of merit to develop. And if the world *has* noticed you publishing the book, I really don't recommend you revise it now. Cut your losses and move on.
- Give up on the book, and on writing. Take a look at the later section 'Throwing in the Towel?'.
- Give up on the book, and write another. Take a look at the later section 'Writing the Next Book'.

Throwing in the Towel?

We writers are a sensitive bunch. We don't like rejection. We don't like critical reviews. We don't like poor sales. Our fragile egos get bruised.

Some authors take it badly when faced with a first book that doesn't do as well as they'd like or expect: 'That's it! I'm done! No more writing! No more books! I've had it with this bloomin' writing business. I'm burning all my notebooks on the fire. I'm donating the laptop to the kids' school. I'm selling my biro collection on eBay. Vegetable gardens, that's the way forward. I'll spend my time tending turnips. *They* don't tell me my characters are one-dimensional. *They* don't criticise my slow pace and tendency to be repetitive. Repetitive, I ask you! Repetitive indeed! That's it. From this day forth I shall cease to be a Writer. I shall be a Vegetable Gardener.'

Oh dear. I come across this kind of reaction quite often in authors. It reminds me a lot of my son George, age three, having a mardy moment: 'Stupid knight! Won't sit on his horse. Sit on it! Argghhhhh! Mummy, I HATE my castle. I HATE this knight. I don't want it any more. I don't like my castle now. I only like my train set. Trains are fun.' The difference is, George quickly calms down and trots back to play with his castle. Because he loves it really. That pesky knight just let him down for a while. But the emotional author may well never get back to writing.

Only you know whether you want to keep writing. If you don't, that's fine. But if you *do* want to write then you have to find a way to move forward from feeling hurt and angry and lacking in confidence.

Ask yourself:

- Are you a writer? Is it a huge part of who you are? Does the idea of not writing any more make you feel sad and lost and empty? Are you prepared to work and work and work at writing?
- Are you happy to stop writing now? Are you glad that you wrote a book, but ready to move on now? Do you want to be a writer a bit, but not that much – not enough to pick yourself up and write some more?

If you decide your book will be your only book then I very much hope you enjoyed the writing process, and I wish you luck in whatever your next endeavour will be.

If you know that you're a writer, pick yourself up, take a deep breath and dive into the next book. Every book you write, you get better. There are plenty of well-known authors out there whose first book has never seen the light of day. Keep at it.

Writing the Next Book

I very much hope that you enjoyed writing your first book – whether you published it or not – and are already itching to write another. It's good news on the creative front, and it's great news in terms of marketability.

The more marketable books you write, the more marketable each book becomes. Here's why:

- You're establishing yourself as a serious author; a brand, if you like. (Chapter 2 contains more info on being a marketable author.)
- Readers assume if you've written more than one book, your first book must have done okay – ergo, you're an okay writer – ergo, they'll give your book a try.
- You're able to cross-market from one book to the other(s). So if a book blogger writes a favourable review of your second book, she's likely to also mention your first book in the review – so she's helping you market both books.

Think of a book series like Harry Potter. If JK Rowling had stopped at *The Philosopher's Stone* (Book 1), that book would be marketable, of course. But as part of a seven-book series, *The Philosopher's Stone* is massively marketable.

But you needn't write a series of books to benefit from having multiple titles within the same genre. For example, say as well as *Writing a Marketable Book* I write *Online Marketing for Authors* and *Inspiration for Writers* and *200 Great Characters in Fiction*. All these books are for the same market – authors – and so they sit nicely side by side.

Remember: The benefit comes when the books are in the same vein and for the same market.

When you're ready to start writing the next book, head back to Chapter 2 and work your way through this book again. This time, you'll find writing a book much easier –

you've learnt a lot, and you've gained confidence that you *can* write a book.

From there, who knows – a third book, a fourth, a fifth. In my experience, writing books can be highly addictive, to the point that my husband has put a sign up in my office that reads *NO MORE BOOKS!* which I cheerfully ignore. Who needs sleep, eh?

In a Nutshell

- Writing isn't a race. Take your time, and care about quality.
- Be a total know-it-all when it comes to the genre in which you're writing.
- Be brutally honest about how your book has done.
- Commend yourself for successes, however small.
- Forgive yourself for mistakes, however large.
- If you've taken your book to agents/publishers and got nowhere, either self-publish or give up on the book.
- If you've self-published your book and it hasn't gone well, either redevelop it or give up on the book.
- Don't quit writing too easily.
- Write another book. Go on. You know you want to…

Notes

Notes

Notes

Notes

Notes

Notes

Notes

Notes

Notes

Notes